My Healing Journey:

Comfort in the Storm

Julie Moment

CONTENTS

PART 2
My Wellbeing Journey

ACKNOWLEDGMENTS

I couldn't have written this book without the help of God who inspired me in the first place and gave me the wisdom to write down my thoughts. I'm thankful to God for always loving me and getting me through everything that life has thrown at me.

I'd also like to thank Jeni for starting editing and Masha Woollard for faithfully volunteering to take over editing my work, correcting my grammatical errors. We got back in touch with Masha as a result of calling on her (when we were out walking near her home) to see if she needed anything during the first lockdown. Many a time I have reached out to bless someone and they have ended up being a blessing to me.

Thank you to my wonderful husband for helping design the cover and self publishing. Also, for standing by me during everything else I've gone through and remaining so positive having the constant faith for my healing and always trusting in God for a good outcome. For having such amazing patience during my breakdown whilst encouraging me day in and day out when we couldn't see any end to it all. Also thank you to him for allowing me to share about our marriage and him as a person in this book. Whatever we have been through I have the reassurance of knowing that my husband is a gift from God. God brought us together and He doesn't make mistakes.

A big thank you to my marvelous parents and sister who supported me during my breakdown and recovery, who never stopped believing in me and never gave up on me. As did my friends Margaret and Ralph Goodenough and Penny and Ian. Thank you especially to my mum for so faithfully phoning me daily for one to two hours at a time when I was in the depths of my suicidal thoughts and anxiety, encouraging me and sacrificing her time for me. She said she wished she could have done more but she has done more than she will ever know. She doesn't acknowledge how amazing she is as a person. She is like 'Wonder Woman' with all that she selflessly does for others. Thank you also to my mum who has understood and believed my struggles in a way that no one else ever could have (apart from those living it) or I don't think ever will apart from God. She has accommodated and understood my limitations and food intolerances. Thank you to Dad for sharing with me his wisdom and his difficulties with hearing loss and tinnitus.

I'm thankful to Penny for being there for me whenever I was in a health crisis. I'm grateful to her and her husband Iain for understanding mental illness and to Penny for taking the time for regularly sending me long encouraging texts. She has a gift from God with words. I also want to thank Penny Martin for allowing me to include the beautiful poems she wrote for me personally.
A big thank you to all those people that prayed for and encouraged me or supported me over the years.

Some of whom I've mentioned above. In Gods family we are there for each other. I'm also thankful for all the excellent Christian teaching and guidance I've received over the years from friends as well as others.

I thank God for the new understanding friends He has miraculously brought into my life since losing my job, Carmen, Denise and Veronica. I thank Veronica for her wonderful company and the inspiring walks we encountered together during lockdown which is how we've become friends. I never thought that God would bring so many wonderful women into my life.

A statement made by Jimi Yates during a conversation we had on messenger, in my opinion, sums my book up very well;

"Your faith and strength of character has been a wellspring of positivity during some testing times."

Introduction

From time to time over the years, I've had thoughts of typing my journey through Chemical Sensitivity and Irritable Bowel syndrome (IBS). Maybe just one or two pages, as I did with some of the testimony relating to my anxiety, but I never got round to it. Then, when thinking about this again in April 2016, all of a sudden it came strongly to my mind to put my health journey into a book. I knew this thought was from God, as normally I would find the thought of writing a book so daunting. But all I felt was excitement. I knew that even though I've struggled with wording and grammar, I didn't need to worry because God would help me. Straight away God gave me the title.

Probably like the majority of people, I didn't appreciate how important it is to have good health until I lost it to the point of struggling to function on an everyday basis. Throughout my life I've suffered from migraines, allergies, anxiety, irritable bowel, chemical sensitivity, a miscarriage, Infertility, hearing loss, depression, anxiety, tinnitus and fibromyalgia.

Christians aren't exempt from suffering and being a Christian doesn't mean you have an easy life. Jesus's life and undeserved suffering on the cross shows us that. Sickness is part of our fallen world.

I've had almost a lifetime of ill health, one thing after another.

This is my personal journey of brokenness to healing, what I've personally learnt over the years and how suffering has developed my faith.

Part 1 describes my health challenges, symptoms, struggles and some coping mechanisms I developed. I've tried to portray an honest and detailed account of how my conditions have affected me on a daily basis.

Part 2 describes my wellbeing journey. I've included how I've invested time in spiritual, physical and mental health that's been worthwhile for healing. I've also described how God has strengthened me, guided me, has given me wisdom and comforted me through all of those trials. Included is a chapter on healing.

The Bible is our rule book for life. I've read it translated as the following (recently learnt it's called an acronym):

> B asic
> I nstructions
> B efore
> L eaving
> E arth.

Putting what it says into practice can alleviates stress, help us cope with problems and improve overall wellbeing.

It was since I gave my life to God and became a Christian that my life took a turn for the better. I suddenly felt as if I'd found life's purpose and a reason for living. It has been a wonderful adventure of my own personal journey with God and the best decision I have ever made. One that I'd never want to change. I discovered a whole new world, God's Kingdom here on earth. The journey has had ups and downs and being a Christian in this world isn't an easy calling. But on the whole, it has been exciting and interesting, full of wonder and mystery. With Christianity there is always something new to discover and learn.

God has walked with me through my journey, helping me to rely on His presence (FROG – fully rely on God) and wisdom every day. The Holy Spirit has always been there ready to help and comfort me, offering me hope in the midst of despair. He has contributed to my healing in a variety of different ways.

Whilst writing this book has also put me on a journey of further self-discovery and revelation. Overall, it has become my journey of wellbeing physically, mentally and spiritually.

Sickness can be frightening, isolating and exhausting. Throughout life I always felt the need to be strong no matter what was going on. I needed to have it all together to support others in my role as a community support worker for eighteen years. After struggling on for many years with various health issues my health journey eventually brought me to place where I value self care more than ever. I've learnt that it's okay not to be okay, it's okay to cry, it's okay to admit I'm struggling or tired. It's okay to take time to myself and not feel guilty about it. And that God isn't all we need but we do at times need someone to talk to but that needs to be the right person. We need to look after ourselves, to cherish ourselves with compassion in order to be at our best to be there for others

I grew up as a very shy and introverted individual with little confidence and self-esteem. However, the faith I found later on in life turned all of that around. I am a very positive and mentally strong person but life happens and a choice I made lead to a breakdown. With support from my family, my faith, sheer will power and strength I fought my way back to good mental health. I feel God has healed me from my breakdown and previous social anxiety to give others hope showing them that you can get through it and can become stronger than ever.

I don't want people to read this and think "poor you." My life hasn't all been doom and gloom. I've had some great times and exciting adventures in my life as well. Sickness doesn't define me. My personality and my identity in Christ are what defines me.

My prayer for this book is that on my journey of openness and vulnerability it will be a source of encouragement to others in some way. I don't claim to have all the answers but my desire is that my own journey and what has worked for me will help others to cope in some way through their own illness, pain and despair.

Because I assume that not everyone who reads this book is familiar with all of the Christian terminology, I feel it's worth giving a few explanations.

Jesus, God and the Holy Spirit are the same. They are The Trinity, three in one. Jesus rose from the dead and is alive and active today, operating on Earth through his Holy Spirit. *'The son is the image of the invisible God, the firstborn over all creation' (Colossians 1:15).* As Christians we believe that everything is directed by God, who governs the whole Earth. However, people have free will and are allowed to make choices.

I also want to give an explanation of Satan, as I will be referring to him from time to time. Satan means adversary or enemy. Satan was an angel who was cast out of heaven so is active in this world, along with his demons. Because Satan hates God and Christians (who love God), he puts negative things in our minds. Good and evil battle against each other (for each individual soul). *"Be alert and of sober mind. Your enemy the devil prowls around like a roaring lion looking for someone to devour"* 1 Peter 5:8. *"The thief comes only to steal and kill and destroy..." John 10:10.* The devil (Satan) is our enemy.

Scriptures quoted are from NIV (New International Version) of the Bible unless otherwise stated.

Part 1
My Health Journey

Allergies

Health problems have been a part of my life since being a child when I suffered regular migraines, which made me lie in bed vomiting and suffering excruciating pain. One of the triggers was being out in the sun which I put down to being blonde with fair skin. While at Secondary School, I remember that I suffered a lot of colds as I often had a runny nose. At the age of eighteen I contracted glandular fever and seemed to struggle with energy levels ever since.

After the dusting and hoovering in my flat, I felt wiped out, and had to sit down and rest. My nose was streaming and I knew something wasn't right. I was reacting to the dust. I mentioned it to my doctor who referred me to the hospital for tests, where I had my arm pricked several times with tiny amounts of things that people are often allergic to. I had two red swollen lumps where they'd put dust and dust mites. This showed I had allergies to these two things. I was also diagnosed with allergic rhinitis and was prescribed a nasal spray to use on a daily basis, which helped a little. Allergic rhinitis is similar to hay fever having the same symptoms.

I felt better for having a diagnosis because even though there wasn't a cure, I was able to look into management techniques. I then bought items such as dust mite bedding cover and an allergy hoover with good filtration to reduce my symptoms.

Even after getting a leather sofa and wooden flooring my symptoms were still severe at times. I recently found out that some of my symptoms are a result of histamine intolerance. This means that for whatever reason my body has too much histamine. Symptoms are reduced by eating a low histamine diet, antihistamines and avoiding triggers. Certain supplements can help.

Anxiety

All my life I felt anxious when in company and in public. There is a difference between worry and anxiety. Anxiety feels more out of control than worry as it produces a feeling of dread that something bad will happen and is often about having a deep-rooted fear of something. However, anxiety can be triggered by worry and worry is given as a definition in the Oxford dictionary. Anxiety causes low self esteem. The symptoms I experienced included intense fear, dread, racing heart, trembling and tension. Until the age of thirty-one, I didn't realise it was social anxiety I was experiencing until I read something explaining this at work in my job as a support worker. Basically, with me it was a fear of people. I hadn't been aware of this until God revealed it to me during my healing. All I knew was that it was a part of me that I'd always lived with so had just learnt to cope with it and get through life the best way I knew how. I persevered in the midst of the fear and tried not to let it hold me back. I had always been shy, sensitive and an introvert and these characteristics can contribute to social anxiety.

People with social anxiety experience emotional distress and anxiety in the following situations:

- being introduced to new people
- making small talk at social events
- being the center of attention (causing you to want to hibernate like an animal)
- meeting people who are in authority
- speaking in a group of people (or to an individual)
- being watched while doing something
- going to work (can cause dread)
- when being criticised and teased
- most social encounters.

Chemical Sensitivity

As an adult I used to get a lot of headaches and feelings of nausea, which I just put down to my dust and dust mite allergies. I sometimes had headaches, similar to migraines, for two or three days at a time. I could be laid up in bed for as long as two or three days in excruciating pain. My sinuses would swell and become very sore.

I suffered fatigue, and had to lie down on the couch to sleep as soon as I got back from work every day. I was very grateful that I only worked six hour days. I wouldn't have been able to hold the job down if I had had to work more hours. I used to fall asleep when travelling anywhere by car, bus, train or plane, except from when I was driving the car, of course. It became a joke with my manager at work that I'd fall asleep even on short journeys. I didn't have a car for many years, which is why I used public transport a lot. Probably just as well. I only managed to miss my destination stop a couple of times. Once was when I was travelling back to Middlesbrough and ended up in Saltburn. As soon as I woke up and realised where I was, I spoke to the driver who didn't seem at all impressed and said, "stay on we are going back". This fatigue caused me and others to believe that I was suffering from ME, or chronic fatigue as it's often called these days.

Sinus infections became a regular occurrence. Doctors repeatedly prescribed antibiotics, which didn't seem to help me at all. When I asked why they weren't working, the doctor stated it was because I needed different antibiotics. When I was researching IBS, information kept coming up about antibiotics playing a part in damaging your gut. Other triggers for gut damage were stress and trauma, which I'd also experienced a lot of in my lifetime. A lot of stress was due to my shyness and anxiety, but other factors played a big part as well.

One day something made me decide to stop using my body spray, then I noticed I had less headaches. I questioned how this could be. I started to research it online and found that there was a name for this condition, whereby people react to the chemicals in products, such as perfumes, cleaning products, air fresheners etc., which was multiple chemical sensitivity (MCS). After all those years of suffering, I was relieved to find a cause for my symptoms. As a result, I decided to try and eliminate chemicals as much as possible, in my home and in my personal hygiene. However, one thing I wasn't able to do was to limit what I was exposed to in the outside world. Every time I ventured out of the house; I was living in fear of becoming ill. I often had to cover my nose with a tissue, especially when using public transport, to prevent me from breathing in the chemicals. The doctors were unable to do anything but prescribe painkillers, informing me it was nothing serious. I desperately wanted answers as to why I was getting these episodes but they were unable to give me any. I was just left to live with it.

I often attended work feeling ill, because if I didn't, I would have had too much sick leave and would have been in fear of losing my job. I'm feeling the emotional pain right now while typing this as it was such a difficult and traumatic time of my life. I reached a point where I was just sick of being ill and in pain. It reached a point where I was ill at work on a weekly basis and I thought I was going to lose my job. However, my manager was very understanding and asked staff not to wear fragrance, bought me an air purifier for the office and supported me with an explanation I wrote to give out to clients. It was a very difficult, stressful, and emotional time of my life.

After years of being ill and then finding out what was causing it, I struggled to go out socially due to the high exposure to peoples' perfumes and after shaves. The only way I could go to Church was to sit right at the back, away from everyone else. I also bought a miniature air purifier that I sometimes wore round my neck.

I didn't want to continue with the way I was living, but unless I isolated myself totally in the house, I had no choice. I reached the point where I bought an air purifier for my home so I could get rid of unwanted chemicals if anyone happened to enter with any on. I avoided social gatherings or anything like that altogether as I just couldn't face the risk of being so ill. I dreaded events such as training at work and in situations like these I prayed that I wouldn't be seated next to anyone wearing strong fragrance. I had to book hair appointments when there was very little chance of any other customers being in the salon, so I didn't get contaminated by hairspray or other hair products. If I attended appointments or visited someone in their home, I had to ask and check that they didn't have plug in air fresheners. I had to remind friends who did have them to switch them off in advance and take them out of the room to clear the air. It wasn't a case of telling people once, they would so easily forget.

Every time I visited my parents before I was aware of the cause, I was ill and my mum said that she must have a really dusty house which I must add wasn't the case. Her home is always spotlessly clean. My mum always kept a plug-in air freshener behind the settee, which I later realised was why I was always ill when I visited. At the time I didn't realise that this was what was causing my headaches.

Before meeting friends and family, I always had to remind them not to wear fragrance. I found that friends wouldn't understand how ill I got as they never saw me when I was at my worst. It would be the next day or two I was laid up in agony in bed, having to take time off work to recover. Most people would think they could get away with just wearing little bit of perfume. I couldn't always smell it due to having a bad sense of smell, which made matters worse. This resulted in a headache coming on before I had a chance to move away from the chemicals. My husband used to be like my little "sniffer dog," telling me if he could smell anything. It was like musical chairs at times. We'd sit down somewhere which was safe for me, then someone would sit next to us that "stank" of perfumes and we'd have to move, then maybe move again. I always said I'd much rather have someone next to me that smelt of body odour than chemicals. Perfumes, aftershave, body spray, etc. were like poison to me.

IBS

I remember one evening, many years ago now, having quite bad stomach pains. A friend informed me it was IBS (irritable bowel syndrome). I continued to have them, on and off, with some other symptoms, which seemed to become more frequent over time. They came on during the night when in bed, then seemed to disappear as soon as I got up. The symptoms were worse around the time of my period. The doctor diagnosed me with IBS and prescribed some medication to reduce spasms in the intestines. These helped at first but eventually I felt no benefit and stopped using them, at which point I was told there was no alternative treatment.

Doctors told me to use painkillers instead, which I used as infrequently as I could get away with, not wanting to cause my body any more damage, I often went to bed with a hot water bottle to soothe my back ache and a heat pad on my tummy. I often had broken sleep due to the intense pain. At no point was I ever given any support on how to manage my symptoms.

The IBS Network states that 'irritable bowel syndrome' or IBS is the name doctors use to describe a collection of otherwise unexplained symptoms relating to a disturbance in the bowels. These include abdominal pain, bloating, constipation and diarrhoea. Pain has always been my worst symptom to cope with, especially when in bed at night. Even though I suffer pain, bloating and constipation, diarrhoea is a symptom I'm thankful I've never had to deal with. I've often thought about those that do have IBS diarrhoea and wondered how difficult it must be to cope with, especially when going out and needing to always be in close proximity of a toilet. Getting the urge and having to go quickly, often accompanies this illness. Thankfully I've only been like that in the morning before leaving for work and then didn't have those symptoms for the rest of the day, which is a blessing when out all day.

In an attempt to reduce my stomach pains my diet became more and more restricted. This has made it difficult for me to eat out, as the majority of dishes on the menu contain an ingredient that I have difficulty tolerating. Chefs tend to cook with a lot of cream, butter, garlic and onions, which are all trigger foods.

If I'm invited out for a meal, I'm often left trying to explain to others why I'm not joining them, questioning how to word it for the best. "I struggle to eat out" didn't seem quite right. "I have food issues" didn't seem quite right either. IBS is such a complex illness to describe to anyone. If anyone asks, I try to keep it simple and just tell them the basics. Unfortunately for me, most socials especially church ones tend to be focused around food or drink these days. Watching what I eat is a stress in itself. Watching what others eat that I'm unable to have sometimes used to make me feel deflated or down but not anymore. Alcohol is an

IBS trigger as it's an irritant to the gut, as is caffeine, so I stopped drinking alcohol and buy decaffeinated and herbal tea bags.

It can be very difficult to put weight on with IBS as fat triggers the symptoms. Also, foods fermenting in the gut can prevent it from being absorbed, which is 'malabsorption'. Therefore, it isn't always what we eat but what we absorb that contributes to our health and weight. I've had people comment on how thin I am or tell me I need to put some weight on, which, given what a struggle it is to gain weight, has been quite hurtful and upsetting for me. Sometimes people just think it's a case of me not eating enough and then start telling me what to eat for weight gain (without knowing my issues), which often consists of junk food. Comments like these made me feel I had to then start explaining why I'm so thin. It can be stressful in itself trying to explain to people what you have and how it affects your life day to day. When I first lost a lot of weight I would just say "it's health related" and try to leave it at that, otherwise it would leave me reliving the difficulties and often trying to explain to someone who still didn't have a clue. I've had to learn to find my own answers to give people, which has been challenging to say the least.

When I tried eating more food, as a result of advice from a concerned friend, my symptoms got worse. Books have suggested to eat little and often, which isn't practical even though I've thought about trying to eat my tea in two portions. This is less possible without the use of a microwave, which I stopped using in an attempt to help reduce the toxic load on my body. Basically, eating is a complex process for me and I manage it the best way I know how, while learning all the time.

After reading 'Cooking for a Sensitive Gut' it helped me understand my condition much better. It explained that some people have a sensitive gut due to inflammation. This causes your gut to be sensitive to food in much the same way as sunburn makes your skin sensitive to the shirt you put on. Any changes or upset can stimulate a sensitive gut. Irritation can be caused by foods such as alcohol, hot spices or bran flakes. Intestinal spasms can affect the gut when we eat fats, coffee, high fibre foods or poorly absorbed carbohydrates called FODMAPS. Fats are one of the most reactive ingredients in a sensitive gut. Stress can make the gut more sensitive to food that stimulates it. Likewise, if we are relaxed, as is often the case when on holiday, our gut becomes less sensitive to foods, which I've found to be the case. Severity of symptoms also depends on amounts of foods eaten. All this explains why some people have said it's impossible to find their triggers.

I'd known for years that I'd be better off not eating wheat in order to reduce my pain but realised that I'd lose weight if I did stop eating it, which given my low weight I couldn't afford to do. I'd made a couple of halfhearted attempts to come off it or cut down but foods tempted me into eating them again, a bit like when someone goes on a slimming diet aiming to lose weight. But I wasn't strong enough to follow it through.

I'd already reduced my dairy consumption to a minimum, in order to reduce my catarrh, which is a symptom of my allergic rhinitis. I started conversing with a Natural Therapist, via e mail, who was on a restricted diet herself for health reasons. Eventually just before Christmas 2014, I knew it was the right time to take on the challenge of cutting out wheat and dairy completely. Bad timing or what! All those lovely foods at my parents' house over Christmas and I was unable to eat a lot of them. And if you have ever been to my mum's house you will be all too familiar with all the different food and cakes she cooks and prepares. After friends of mine visited their comment was, "what a feast". My health had also forced me to cut several other foods out of my diet.

I was told my stomach pains could be due to gluten but not just traditional gluten - oats, rice and all grains, which would include cutting out gluten free bread. The thought of an even more restricted diet and losing even more weight when I'd already dropped to a size 6 in clothes, caused me to slump into a depression, which lasted over a year, up until the beginning of 2016. At times I was in a very dark place, just wanting to be taken up to heaven to be with Jesus. Thinking about it now, to my surprise, antidepressants didn't even cross my mind. I managed to get through it all with God's help. I was living in fear, fear of losing more weight, fear of how food was damaging my body, fear of the unknown, fear of my illness becoming worse, fear of being on an even more restricted diet, you name it. Fear was the cause of my depression that lasted over a year. I'd allowed the enemy to have control of my mind. This depression caused me more problems than enough. I stopped being able to socialise with friends or go for days out, I became withdrawn and found it very difficult to make conversation with people, I was unable to go on holiday with my husband, my energy levels decreased even further and I just wanted to be at home in my own little world.

After I was healed from the depression, I noticed my aches and pains reduced dramatically, and I realised that the depression had made them worse. It's something that's common with depression due to reduced serotonin levels (the happy hormone). I surprised myself that even though it was a struggle, I was able to remain at work and do my job. No one at work seemed to be aware of my depression as they didn't know me before that, but I was probably good at covering it up as well and just getting on quietly with my job.

I had never been happy with my usual size eight figure; I felt skinny and always desired and strived to put on weight. What most women would give to be a size eight! I'd say that how difficult it is for people to lose weight it's as difficult as that for me to put it on. I've now been able to come to terms with it as God made me slim anyway and there isn't a lot, I can do about it. As my dad says I've got his genes. The way I look at it now is that as long as I have enough health and energy to enjoy life, I'm happy with my weight. It's only by God's grace that I have these things.

At church in 2012, when I went forward for prayer for my IBS, God spoke to me via my swallow necklace. The lady praying for me said I should soar like the swallow when I have the energy but rest in God when I haven't. Basically, God was telling me to listen to my body. She said that swallows fly in the thermals where air rises due to heat, which is similar to how God will enable me to soar in the Holy Spirit. She said to let God heal me in his timing and at his pace, don't force it. After living with health problems for so many years and thinking thoughts like, "will I ever be free from these symptoms" it's been such a challenge not to try and find healing through different avenues.

However, placing all of my attention on striving and trying to be well has often taken my attention away from what God wants to do and what He is doing. My heart often grew heavy with negative thoughts, worry, fear and doubt. There are times when I've been consumed with hopelessness, feeling weak, helpless and powerless, short tempered and wondering why God hadn't responded to my cries for help. There have been times when I've felt all alone. It's easy to feel that God has abandoned us if we can't feel his presence. However, we have to not go by our feelings, remembering that he says in Deuteronomy 31:6 that He will never leave us or forsake us. Jesus was right by my side all the time with his Holy Spirit living in me. Even when we can`t see it, God is at work, answering our prayers. Things can be happening that we are unaware of and unable to see. All things are under God`s control and according to His will.

Miscarriage

In 2008, despite my health issues, and after much debating and discussion, my husband and I decided to try for a baby. About one month later I started with what I thought was my period and when I went to the toilet, I lost a small blood clot. This was unusual and abnormal for me, so I decided to see the doctor who reassured me that it can happen sometimes and it was nothing to worry about. I went away feeling reassured thinking nothing more about it.

However, I started getting soreness in my stomach, so went back to see a different doctor who told me that if I was bleeding, I wasn't pregnant. I continued feeling unwell and became so fearful, wondering what could be wrong with me. I had symptoms of tiredness, lack of energy and an inability to walk fast. The soreness started turning into pain. When I mentioned this to a friend, her opinion was that I was pregnant. Another friend asked me, "you aren't pregnant, are you? Your boobs have got bigger".

I then saw an advert for a pregnancy test at the chemist near the place where I worked so I popped in to ask for one. The Pharmacist also doubted I could be pregnant, so I went away without the test, again feeling reassured. However, the pain was continuously getting worse and I was still bleeding. This lasted for eighteen days altogether, at which point I visited the doctors again.

The doctor then decided to arrange for me to have a pregnancy test. When the nurse told me that the results were positive, I just burst into tears because I could sense there was something wrong. The nurse made me go back in to see the doctor who informed me I could be having an ectopic pregnancy. This meant that the foetus was in the fallopian tube, not in the womb. Therefore, there was a high risk of death to the foetus and a potential threat to my health. As a result, the doctor admitted me straight to hospital. The fear and anxiety I had escalated as I was petrified of operations. I took an overnight bag but was seen in accident and emergency, checked over, told that the pain I was having could be normal and two hours later was sent home.

The pain started getting so bad that I was unable to lie down or sleep at night. Therefore, I was then admitted to the gynaecology ward at the hospital for investigations. Having to go into hospital was a fearful and anxious experience. I was anxious, not only about operations but also about my chemical sensitivity and the fear of being ill. I dreaded being put into a room with other people, as I knew I would become ill as a result of the beauty products they used.

I was praying and doing my best to relax as much as I could, when the next morning a woman sprayed a lot of body spray. I spoke to the nurse and explained my concerns but I was told that there weren't any single rooms free. Therefore, I had to find refuge in the day room.

After sitting there for a while, I wandered down the corridor and found an empty room with a bed. I took the opportunity to use it, informing the staff where I was. I was so relieved that I thanked God for that room! The nurse on duty approached me in the room and told me abruptly that she couldn't keep walking down the corridor to keep an eye on me, so if I needed anything I'd have to come to the desk. I was happy with that. However, I was anxious about having to go back to that other shared room to sleep the night. With chemical sensitivity not being a recognised illness in the UK, people didn't understand it and I was made to feel, even by the medical profession, as if it was all imaginary or psychological. When I told professionals that I had multiple chemical sensitivity I was left having to explain what it was, which then just got dismissed and often not even taken seriously.

Two friends came to visit me in hospital during the day when I was alone. I hadn't seen my friend Penny for a while but she had found out from another friend that I was in hospital and said that she couldn't let me go through something like this on my own. Penny asked the nurse if there was any possibility of the baby still being alive, to which she replied "yes". My friends took the opportunity to pray over me, which couldn't have happened if I'd still been in the room with others. The company of other Christians and prayers lifted my spirits somewhat. My wonderful parents also came straight over to see me after they'd finished work. After a couple of hours of being in that room, the nurse informed me that a room had become free that I could move into. I was so grateful for that room.

As it happened, I was discharged that evening on condition that I had someone with me all the time as the doctors weren't sure whether it was an ectopic pregnancy or if I was going to have a miscarriage. My husband couldn't be with me during the day, as he had to be at work, so my wonderful mum drove back all the way (one and half hours) from Scarborough to Middlesbrough, where I lived, to be with me. I had to keep going for regular blood tests to the hospital and I eventually realised that the small blood clot I'd initially lost must have been the miscarriage, which explained the resulting pain. I couldn't help but think all the trauma could have been avoided if someone had known that in the first place.

God can speak to us through any person or situation. God comforted and strengthened me through the following words the day I was admitted to hospital through a song I heard on the radio, 'everything is going to be alright'.

Two days later at Church, Ann, when asking my husband how I was, turned a piece of paper over and it said; *'Trust in God, everything is going to be alright.'*

Three days later Ann phoned me with the song words; *'put thou thy trust in God, how wise, how strong His hand.'*

The next day I felt God saying to me*: 'I'm strengthening you because I have a plan for you.'* Difficult and traumatic life experiences change us by making us stronger, wiser and more equipped to help others.

Because I'd become pregnant once, I didn't have any doubts in my mind that it would happen again. When we moved, we bought a three bedroomed house, so there was an extra room for a baby when we had one.

Infertility

The process of struggling to conceive is difficult when what you envisioned isn't going to plan. Having to have sex at set times of the month killed the passion and put a strain on our relationship. I researched ways of increasing my chances of getting pregnant, and remember holding my legs in the air for a long time after sex due to claims that more sperm would reach where it needed to be. I can laugh about it now. Not being able to conceive can make some women feel like they are less of a woman, but they're not.

Since attending the Fertility Clinic, I became extremely stressed with it all and emotionally drained from all the struggling, treatments, emotional pain etc. I finally learnt not to beat myself up over it and leave it with God, trusting that if it was meant to be, it would happen. I had had enough of it and needed to move on. I learnt to trust in God whatever the outcome.

After this point, I had well meaning people, who never thought to ask what I wanted, tell me they would pray for me to conceive. Often people pray in the way they think things should go, rather than asking you where you're at and how you'd like them to pray for you. It's a mistake we can be all guilty of.

I had a word from a Christian saying that he felt God was telling him I was going to conceive. Now, I have no doubt that if God gave me a baby, he would enable me to cope and it would be a blessing for us. But, at that point, being almost forty seven years old at the time, the thought of it filled me with dread. We had moved on from wanting children and were enjoying our life fully as it was. I've also been told that it isn't right to believe that God wouldn't want us to have children because that isn't His plan for our lives. I personally believe that God wouldn't want us to have what we don't desire.

Since reading up about how different forms of contraception can have a negative impact on your body and health, not having to use any is one good thing that's come out of all this.

Even though I'd never strongly desired a child or been very maternal, the thought of not being able to have one was a very emotional journey and difficult to come to terms with. I experienced feelings of letting my husband down, but it helped me knowing that he already has a son of his own from his previous marriage.

At times, in situations when I'd least expect it, I would become very upset and emotional. I supported a pregnant woman at work during her scan when she was told that they were unable to find the baby`s heartbeat. At this time, I was strong for her and didn't show any signs of upset. However, it was emotional for me to be in a room with a new born baby. The times when I felt emotional pain were unpredictable and didn't always make sense to me.

I found it particularly difficult when I learned that my sister had accidentally become pregnant. It was even more of challenge when it was expected that I would hold the newborn baby infant in a room full of people. My newly born nephew was being passed round and when it was said that I was next I didn't know what else to do but to make a quick exit for fear of breaking down crying in front of everyone. My sister was totally understanding when she realised what was happening and proceeded to pray for me when we were alone.

I felt that the best way to deal with new baby situations was to distance myself from them as much as possible because that made it far easier for me to bear. However, these situations couldn't be totally avoided. This would have meant not being with family at Christmas, which is a tradition we have always practiced. I often found myself surrounded by babies in church meetings and ended up supporting a client at work with a baby.

God has blessed me along my journey by putting me in touch with other women who have also been unable to conceive. It made me feel that I wasn't alone and it helped to know that there were others who could identify with how I was feeling.

I remember once, when we were at New Wine Christian Camp, and I was on the prayer ministry team. One evening we were asked to sit near where the mothers were with their babies and young children. It didn't even cross my mind that I wouldn't be able to cope with the situation, but I ended up being very upset. However, releasing emotions is a good thing as this is God's way of healing us. The pain comes to the surface and is dealt with rather than being repressed or buried inside. I was feeling very nervous, whilst waiting to be prayed for. A lady that I was familiar with, who was heading up our prayer team, came over to me and asked what was wrong. When I told her, she said, 'you are looking at someone who wasn't able to have any children.' You have no idea how comforted that made me feel. She went on to say that she'd become a grandmother through her step son and that was something I could also hope for as my husband also had a son.

As humans we want to make sense of things. I searched for clues that might make some sense of my infertility and make it easier for me to cope. There can be a lot of unanswered questions. Was God not allowing me to have a baby because He knew I wasn't well enough to look after one? Whether it was the case or not, I clung to this and made it my reason why I was unable to conceive, as it eased the pain. My mum said she was concerned that if we did have a baby, I would need a lot of help.

I wondered what I should or could have done differently that might have prevented the miscarriage. At first, I blamed myself for taking strong painkillers regularly, thinking that was what caused it. However, a lovely nurse in the hospital reassured me that this wasn't the case. Five days after coming out of hospital when I put the radio on, the first words of a song were '*it's not easy to understand it*'. It wasn't until years later when I was reading information about hypothyroidism (underactive thyroid), which I was also diagnosed with later in life, that I learnt what doctors and consultants either don't know or fail to tell you.

Hypothyroidism (underactice thyroid) can make it difficult to get pregnant and cause infertility. I read it's one of the most common causes of infertility. It can reduce the number of eggs being released, which the Fertility Clinic found to be my problem. It's due to hypothyroidism causing hormone problems. I also read that studies have shown that women with hypothyroidism who are pregnant have an increased risk of having a miscarriage. Previously, I'd just put my infertility problem down to my age but having more answers helped me to feel so much better about things.

After the miscarriage occurred the possibility that we might never be able to have any children didn't even cross my mind.

Hearing Loss

I first realised that I was losing my hearing in my thirties when I'd been on the phone for an hour and my arm was aching and I changed hands as well as ears to continue the conversation. The sound was so much quieter in my left ear. That's when I decided to have a hearing test at Boots, where I was told to go and see my GP. I was then sent to audiology at the hospital for another hearing test. They told me they could give me a hearing aid but because I was managing ok, I declined the offer.

It wasn't until several years later when I realised, I'd reached a point where I was missing a lot of what was being said at work, especially in meetings and training. Colleagues frequently laughed when my manager was stood next to me and I was busily typing unaware of him speaking to me. Thankfully I saw the funny side too. I believe it's my sense of humour that has helped me cope better in certain situations. My hearing problems caused me stress at work. There were small changes I could make to manage it such as sending e mails at times instead of talking to someone on the phone, go into a quiet room to make a call if the office was too loud (that's if a room was available). However, there was no getting away from the fact that I still had to struggle with hearing and the added fatigue that it brings.

History shows that deaf people have been viewed as being less intelligent than hearing people. The statement I've seen used is 'deaf not stupid' which in my view sums it up well. One in five people in the UK have some form of permanent hearing loss. It's most probably many more than that due to some not having been diagnosed. I've come across several people who make it obvious they don't hear what people are saying. But how do you tell someone they can't hear? Hearing loss has been described by someone as making a call when you have a bad mobile connection. I thought this to be an exceptionally good explanation as it can be about clarity not volume. Another description of hearing loss is that it's like being under water.

It's interesting that even our spouses we have been married to for years forget about our hearing loss and try making conversation whilst walking away, talking from another room or looking the other way. After fifteen years this is still a regular occurrence with us. I remember my dad telling me that when he was attending an appointment with the audiologist, she asked him what his problem was. He replied, 'it's my wife. She talks to the cupboard!'. I stuck notes in the cupboard and dishwasher saying, "don't talk to me I can't answer you, speak to your wife". It helps relieve stress if we can make a joke of it and give ourselves a laugh.

I found myself missing my telephone appointment with Social Services due to my husband forgetting to wake me. As a result, I have been provided not only with the loop system for the television, but also a travel alarm clock that goes under my pillow and flashes and vibrates and a tinnitus machine that plays various sounds. I no longer have to rely on my husband to wake me.

Due to me missing information during team meeting and group training I decided to ask my GP for a referral for another hearing test. As a result of the test, I was informed I required two hearing aids. In one way it seemed inevitable, as hearing problems run in both sides of my parent's family. Unfortunately, due to the nature of my hearing loss I had to have the ones that came with ear moulds and big tubes. My only consolation was that I had long hair which I always wore down over my ears, so I didn't need to worry about people seeing them or having to think about a different hair style. I'd never been one for wearing my hair up due to having very large ears, which is a characteristic that affects some of my dad's side of the family. Even though no one could see the hearing aids, except when I went out in the wind, I still like many people do, felt embarrassed and self conscious about having to wear them. I can't understand why many people wear glasses without an issue but find having to wear hearing aids embarrassing and often feel the need to hide them.

The first thing I said to the audiologist who fitted my hearing aids was, "What's that noise?" He replied, "It's the clock." I was shocked at how loud it was. I was told to just use them at home at first for one hour, each day increasing it gradually by an hour at a time.

I remember hearing something in the house and asking my husband what the loud noise was. He told me it was the fridge freezer. I said, "It's so loud, how do you cope with that?" When I was cooking, it sounded like a tornado!

The first time I went out with my aids in to my Pilates class, I was disorientated whilst trying to figure out what all the new noises were. During the Pilates session, I could hear every little sound of every movement that people made on the mats. The noise of everyone talking before it started was overwhelming, as it was at church.

At church it felt deafening when everyone clapped. Peoples' whispers behind me felt as if they were coming from inside my head, so did my voice when I was speaking. The new noises were overwhelming. The peaceful world I used to live in was totally disrupted. At times my brain felt overloaded, making me want to rip the hearing aids out. High pitched noises were the worst, such as the sound of cutlery rattling in the drawer or children screaming. I had a friend who had a high-pitched laugh, bless her, and I often did have to rip my hearing aid out when I was with her.

No one had ever prepared me for the shock of the whole experience. As my brain adjusted to new noises, some of them became quieter but others still cause me problems. It's because hearing aids amplifying all sounds, including noises you don't want to hear, such as background noise. They increase sensitivity to loud noises by making things louder but not always clearer.

One of the most difficult tasks was learning to speak on the phone with them in. I remember when I used to phone my Auntie Barbara, she would say, "Just a minute, let me take my hearing aid out." She could hear better without it which made me laugh. But I can understand that now. I've heard, it's a common practice for people to use the phone without them, but I had no choice but to persevere with them in as I relied on using the phone a lot in my job. Otherwise, I'd be forever taking them in and out then running the risk of losing them.

It was a challenge to hear over the background noise, as it was more amplified through a microphone. I had to learn my own ways of coping such as turning the left aid off whilst using the phone in my right ear (the one I could hear best with) or taking myself into another room where it is quiet when phoning.

It didn't help that I got my hearing aids fitted not too long before Christmas as the cafes I met clients in for work were packed out. Phone calls in these places are almost, if not completely, impossible. Keeping Support Sessions at work to a minimum of one hour whenever possible, helped me manage the stress and tiredness of concentrating to hear. Work provided me with a mobile phone especially designed for people with hearing difficulties, which made a massive difference but I still struggled so much that I was given an appointment to see the Hearing Therapist at the hospital.

The Hearing Therapist informed me that I needed to retrain my brain to block out the background noise, which could take several weeks. She gave me an exercise to carry out every day, but eventually things just started to improve naturally. The therapist said it didn't help that I was under a lot of stress due to other events in my life, as stress reduces your ability to hear.

My nineteen-year-old cat was very ill and we eventually made the decision to have him put to sleep. But it was such a blessing to be able to actually hear him eating and drinking, something I had previously missed. Your brain isn't used to all the new and different sounds from what you normally hear. The brain has to retrain itself and that can be very tiring. Even now I hate the noise at times, as there seems to be so much of it. For this reason, some don't use their aids at home.

The therapist also gave me some good tips, things I'd never thought of such as when I'm in public places making sure I sit with my back to a wall so I aren't picking up noise from behind me. It's common sense when you think about it but interesting how sometimes these things need to be pointed out to you.

My job as a support worker was all about communicating with people. I was never told that getting used to hearing aids could be as difficult as it was for me. It's something you have to persevere with. I can totally understand why so many people give up on them too early as they feel they can't cope with the change.

Even though I thank God for hearing aids as I can hear people that I couldn't otherwise hear, as you can see there is a downside to wearing them. The whole experience was extremely stressful. At least I had the comfort of knowing that when I was at home, I could take them out if I wanted to and just sit peacefully. That was before the tinnitus came along. I enjoyed doing this when my husband was watching something on TV I wasn't interested in, which means I hardly had to hear it.

Background noise can be so loud it makes it so difficult to hear the people next to me. I feel people could think I'm staring at them when I try to read lips which I automatically fell into doing before I got the aids.

When I forgot to take my aids to work one day it reminded me of how much not being able to hear can knock your confidence. I was trying to speak to people as little as possible in case I wasn't able to hear what they said in return.

One thing I became aware of is how much ignorance there is about hearing problems within the hearing community. It is one of the most misunderstood disabilities. Some people think that, because you have your hearing aids in, you can hear perfectly. When I couldn't hear at work, colleagues would ask if I had my hearing aids in. However, hearing aids can't give you back the hearing you've lost, but just amplify the sounds you can still hear.

I've been put off telling people that I have hearing aids due to their shock of thinking that I'm too young as they think it`s only a disability that occurs with old age. However, being more open with people about my hearing loss, has helped me to accept the problem.

Later I was told the extent of my struggles with my hearing aids was because I waited until my hearing was unmanageable before getting my hearing aids, which apparently makes it more difficult adjusting to them. So, if you are reading this and you are thinking of getting your ears tested, please, don't let my experiences put you off as it's great just being able to hear things you couldn't hear before and you do learn to manage the difficulties that come with hearing aids.

Struggling to hear is made worse by people's inability to communicate clearly and effectively. Unfortunately, many people mumble, don't pronounce their words clearly or talk with their hand over their mouth. Others shout which distorts the sound. I feel education is not only required to teach people about deafness but also about communication skills. It's a discussion I had with my dad, who is left with only part hearing in one ear, therefore, it must be a lot more frustrating for him than for me. It's been helpful being able to talk with my dad who understands all the difficulties associated with hearing loss and hearing aids due to his own personal struggles. However, like with everything everybody's experience is different.

I attended an "dealing with deafness" week arranged by DDS (Durham Deafened Support). It taught us that people lose different parts of their hearing, for example I can hear high pitched noises better but some people may hear lower tones better. This is something I'd not thought about before, even though I was using high pitched ring tones on all my phones and doorbell.

The week at DDS taught me to have the confidence to speak up when I can`t hear people. However, I found this did not usually have a lasting effect. There can also be a cost to speaking out. Why does it always have to be foreign people or those with accents who seems to phone from Virgin, Sky or wherever it may be? I find myself informing them I'm struggling to hear because I'm hard of hearing or I tell them I have a hearing loss. The majority of the time, sooner or later they hang up.   To me it highlights peoples lack of patience with those who have a disability. I'm usually happy to have got them off the line so quickly. My husband told me he will try that one next time someone phones who he doesn't want to speak to.

One thing asked on the DDS "dealing with deafness" week was, "Who hasn't experienced depression as a result of their hearing problem?" I was the only one able to say I'd got through it without any depression, which was only due to me being a Christian and having God in my life to help me through.

It was pointed out that tiredness is an issue as working hard and using more concentration to hear is tiring for your brain. The term used is concentration fatigue. It can be hard work, especially when people talk fast, have an accent or a very softly spoken voice. A 2003 work-life study performed in Sweden revealed that people with hearing loss felt exhausted more often after a regular working day than did hearing people.

Lipreading classes proved to be very beneficial. I found an excellent teacher online. I didn't realise how complex hearing is until it was explained to us. When one of us gets a word wrong she explains the reasoning behind it and it makes complete sense. It all comes down to the lip pattern and how different letters and words look when put together. I find it fascinating. However, we were told that only about 30% can be lipread and extra information is needed in order to understand what is being talked about.

I recently had another hearing test in 2021 to find that my hearing had deteriorated which is usually the case when you live with hearing loss. I wasn't surprised as having the noise of tinnitus also makes it more difficult to hear. As a result, I was informed that the domes that go into my ears that I'd progressed to as technology advanced were insufficient now for my level of hearing loss therefore, I would require the molds again. They take an impression of your ear then make the molds accordingly. However, they caused open sores that then took over a week to heal. After this occurred twice, they decided to look at a different style of mold. I learnt something new as I didn't know there were several styles of ear molds. Molds trap the sound in more which is why they are used in cases of more advanced hearing loss.

Thyroid

For the majority of the time, I currently do well and cope with my hypothyroidism (underactive thyroid). Mornings can be difficult when I wake up feeling stiff, tired, in pain and lacking in motivation. Once I'm out of bed, knowing I have a mission to go to work or whatever else I have to accomplish, it doesn't take me long to get going. I have days when I have muscle pains and weakness which can contribute to me feeling more stressed and irritable. However, because hypothyroidism and fibromyalgia have similar symptoms it's difficult to identify what symptoms are related to which condition. Weekends were worse after a week at work and Sunday afternoons had become a routine of falling asleep on the settee if I didn't fall asleep at church first.

Hypothyroidism causes everything in the body to slow down. Therefore, the immune system is sluggish and slow to respond to infection. I seem to pick up everything there is going and often get things worse than the majority. I read that glandular fever can cause damage to the thyroid which I had in my late teenage years. My energy levels haven't been the same since.

There can be an emotional side to any illness. I experienced a variety of emotions, thoughts and feelings. I was left to cope with misunderstanding from friends, colleagues, relatives and even other Christians. What can't be seen can be very difficult for others to understand. 'Invisible Illness' is the term used to describe any illness that can't be visibly seen. "You look really well," people say to me. This had a positive effect on me and gave me hope, but for some it could have a negative effect causing them to think people don't believe they are ill or they are exaggerating it.

I thought that if I was starting to look really well then maybe that was the start of God healing me or a result of all my clean eating and none toxic lifestyle. Well, a reduced toxic lifestyle, as no one can be completely toxic free in this day and age. I had people who tried to get me to eat something that would later cause me a lot of stomach pain. Another person advised me to take painkillers, then I could eat whatever I wanted. I refused to be on painkillers constantly, putting more chemicals into my body. I also had people who told me to pray over my food before eating it, meaning that if I did this, then the food wouldn't cause me any problems. I replied, "It doesn't work like that, I wish it did." Didn't they think I'd tried that one?

Foot

In 2017, once I accepted that I was going to be off work for six weeks with a broken foot, I started thinking about all the things I could do, such as paint the fence. However, I didn't realise how difficult it would be to get around. Whenever I did anything, such as getting up and dressed, I was exhausted. My muscles were aching with putting all the weight on the one leg and my hands were sore with using the crutches. Unless you've experienced a broken bone, you can't identify with all the draw backs and emotions it presents.

I then thought of a good idea and asked my husband to bring the computer chair down from upstairs. I was then able to whizz around the kitchen on it whilst cooking and down the hall way to the lounge and toilet. It took some pressure off my hands. It also meant that I could carry things on my lap.

However, I still had to use the crutches quite a bit and felt as if I would get blisters if I continued with them much longer. I then had an idea to phone the Occupational Therapy department for some advice, who put me on to another service who said they would deliver me some different crutches. These had hand rests on and were much easier on the palms of my hands.

A week later we ended up without a bathroom for over one week as it had already been planned for that date well in advance. I kept being told by my husband; it wasn't good timing for the breaking of my foot. However, as everyone knows things like that aren't planned and we got on with it the best way we could. My husband was doing all the work on the bathroom and whilst he was demolishing everything in there, the ceiling collapsed. He then found all the floorboards needed replacing as they had all rotted. All the pipework also needed replacing. Until you uncover things you don't always know the extent of the work. I prayed for my husband every day and one thing I prayed for was supernatural energy and he ended up working all day up until nine o'clock in the evening. Over a week later we still didn't have a bathroom and I'm not saying this because he's a slow worker but he is a thorough perfectionist. He also had to keep going to shops for supplies. At that point my dad asked me if it was looking nice to which I laughed and replied that the floorboards are nice and the plastering too.

One morning my husband came into the kitchen and asked, "How are you doing, my love?" That morning I quoted my post on Facebook: "well, no bathroom, a broken foot, no hot water, but I'm counting my blessings. We have a kettle to boil the water in, a sink to get washed in, a downstairs toilet and a bed settee downstairs to sleep on. And best of all it's only temporary. We are blessed to have clean running water, not having to carry water from a river like many people do." We were able to have a good laugh about it. I felt I was able to cope better with the no bathroom situation than I would have done if I was still at work. I took it in my stride because I didn't have to rush to be anywhere.

After three weeks of coping with crutches, my plaster cast was exchanged for a boot that came up to my knee. I enjoyed the freedom of not having to use the crutches, which made it so much easier to be able to carry things. The boot wasn't easy to walk in and was so heavy, but I was glad to have it and be able to walk even if it meant I was much slower and unable to go far.

A few days of using the boot, when I was feeling sorry for myself due to swelling, aching and soreness of my ankle and sole of my foot, I read something that made me think about my thoughts. I realised that I needed to start meditating on what was good about my situation and praise God for those things. This changed my perspective and lifted me up. I was praying every day, speaking to my foot and bone to be healed in Jesus' name. Answers to prayer are achieved through the power of Jesus; it has nothing to do with ourselves. I thanked God for my foot and believed that everything was going to be alright.

One evening, I was hobbling round the supermarket with my husband, when I happened to bump into a colleague I worked with. I was in great discomfort trying to get around with the boot on, using the crutches. After we'd chatted, she asked, "You must be fed up, aren't you?" It was said more like a statement as if she expected me to be fed up. My answer was, "No, I'm ok." Afterwards, when I thought about it, it felt almost right to think that under the circumstances, I should have been fed up. I'm a person who likes to get out to things that are going on in the community. However, I wasn't even able to make it into town on the bus or even to a prayer and worship time that a friend had offered to take me to. It should have bothered me that I was isolated in the house but it didn't. In fact, it was just the opposite. I was enjoying it. I didn't know where the days went, as they just went so fast. Why wasn't I fed up? There was only one explanation for it and that was God. God had turned the situation around and enabled me to feel at peace with the situation and all my restrictions. Because I was focused on God and trusting in him, he kept me at peace. '*You will keep in perfect peace all who trust in you, all whose thoughts are fixed on you.' (Isaiah 26:3 NLT)*.

One other thing, that helped me on my journey, was the knowledge that others were also struggling with a broken foot at the same time. I'm part of a Gluten Free Group on Facebook where someone posted a picture of the foot they had broken. I sent them a friendly message and said that I would pray for good and fast healing. Then someone else put a photo of their foot in a boot stating they had broken theirs a week ago. Little did I know that a few days later, it was going to be me who needed all the prayers I could get for my foot. We checked how each other was doing and occasionally sent a little friendly supportive message. At least I was able to let them know I was thinking of them and praying for them.

One thing I noticed since breaking my foot was the unusual constant lack of energy and tiredness I was coping with every day. One of the other women said she was experiencing the same thing and put it down to the healing process and coping with walking with the boot on. I did wonder myself whether it was the reason. However, the biggest struggle of this whole experience was when I thought I was going to get back to work after the seven weeks, to find out that wasn't possible. I began realising that the soreness I had when attempting to walk in the boot was the same symptoms as when I was told I had Planter Fasciitis. Planter Fasciitis is damage to the ligament running along the sole of your foot, causing heel pain, progressing to sole pain.

The consultant was surprised I turned up to my appointment using crutches when I had the boot on. I told him about my symptoms. His response was to advise me to walk on it without the boot. However, the more I used my foot standing or walking (I didn't walk far), the more painful it became, to the point where I was unable to walk on it at all. Planter Fasciitis is more common than I realised. I was surprised how many people have either experienced it or heard of someone who's had it. I had a GP appointment to confirm this diagnosis. After sorting a Physiotherapy referral, myself, they gave me a telephone appointment informing me that Planter

Fasciitis was the combination of several factors as a result of the fracture. One of those was the fact that I have flat feet and hadn't been able to use my insoles for arch support that I always used in my footwear. I was still unable to use them due to the pain they caused when having them in my shoes. At times I was unable to bear my shoes on and even socks that had patterns on the bottom.

I waited to speak to the Physiotherapist before doing any of the exercises for Planter Fasciitis as I didn't want to make anything worse due to the fracture. She said it was fine to go ahead with the exercises. I didn't experience any pain during the exercises but after two days I was unable to walk for three and a half days. My symptoms flared up worse and I had pain and shooting pains where I hadn't had pain before. I feared the worst, fearing that I'd done some lasting damage. Anxiety kept hitting me. I was back to praying against it. Thankfully my symptoms had started to ease off and the GP confirmed I hadn't done any lasting damage. However, it was a challenge being on and off the crutches as symptoms flared and then eased off. I began feeling I'd overstretched a muscle. My other foot was sore with taking most of the impact. I couldn't even get to the corner shop, which is usually a five-minute walk away.

During this time, I really had to stay close to God. I was upset and frustrated that I was unable to get back to work. When I told another Christian that I was concerned about getting back to work, she said,

"You know that God said, "Don't be anxious about anything". What this lady said reminded me to talk to God about my concerns. I was then able to give it to God by saying, "If you want me back to work, heal this foot!" One thing I learnt from this part of my journey was how to identify with some elderly and disabled people who struggle to get about.

When I couldn't leave the house due to my fracture, I accepted it, but when I was unable to walk anywhere due to the foot pain, it was much more of a challenge. It's not that I needed to go out as my husband did all the shopping or I accompanied him. In my wisdom, the next time I went shopping, I tried out the mobility trolly rather than wearing myself out with the crutches, but it took much longer and wasn't easy. It made me realise how much of a struggle it is for those, who for whatever reason have mobility problems and don't even have access to a mobility scooter or a car. I was unable to drive or even walk to the doctors who are about a ten minute walk away from my home. I was left wondering who I could phone to give me lift. Thankfully I had a friend and a colleague who helped out.

Two weeks after the first attempt to carry out the exercises, the doctor advised me to start up the exercises again. I took it very gently this time, but regardless of this, I started getting shooting pains in the night and then was in so much pain again. When I saw the doctor, she felt my foot and just focused on pain relief. All I wanted to know was what I had done to it and what I needed to do to get better. I was told to rest but walk on it if that makes sense. So that's what I did. I felt that some surrounding tissues had been damaged as a result of my accident.

I began experiencing a whole host of symptoms in both my feet including aching and weakness in my ankle, tingling, heel and sole pain. In the injured foot I also got shooting pains and what felt like little electric shocks. It was a frightening experience and an extremely challenging time to cope with. At times like these the worst thoughts can go through your mind. I clung to God for comfort. *'When doubts filled my mind, your comfort gave me renewed hope and cheer,' (Psalm 94:19 NLT.* God then gave me renewed hope. My struggles increased my faith and brought me closer to God.

I felt some guilt with being off work for so long as it was leaving the office short staffed. I was now on my tenth week off, however, I'm aware that God doesn't want us to feel guilt. It had been at the back of my mind for a while to wonder if I would be able to get back to work but God has our best interests at heart and he knows what's best for us in the long term. So, I repented of the guilt, prayed and trusted in God.

Mental Breakdown

During December 2018 I decided to see an Osteomyologist (similar to an Osteopath), in the hope that it would reduce my ongoing shoulder and neck pain. Osteomyologists manipulate your body in order to try and improve injuries or pain. I had prayed on and off for years about the pains. A couple of colleagues at work had been to similar therapists and had positive results. So, I started thinking about it and I thought, "it can't do any harm to try it". The pains could be disabling and incapacitating at times but there were periods of time where I didn't have any at all. I'd already tried Physiotherapy and other techniques. I persevered through the anxiety I felt whilst at the appointment, as I was so desperate to get better or just have a reduction in my pain that caused excruciating headaches.

Often it can be so easy to take matters into our own hands if we feel that God isn't doing anything to help us. Scripture tells us to persevere in prayer, but for how long? The thing is; God's timing is different to our timing. We want things now and His timing can be years later. It reminds me of the story of Sarah and Abraham in the Bible.

Sarah was unable to conceive and God promised them a baby at the age of ninety. They grew tired of waiting so Abraham decided to sleep with their slave woman and she became pregnant. Later God fulfilled his promise to them but they hadn't waited for his timing. Waiting can make you feel that God has forgotten you. You start wondering if God will ever answer your prayer. Sometimes He answers in ways we don't expect, for example; when I prayed for healing from the chemical sensitivity and God provided a lady who told me about some supplements to take that took it away. God used that lady and the supplements as part of my healing.

The Osteomyologist appointments weren't pleasant to say the least. He told me to undress and left the room where I was left standing in my underwear feeling confused and wondering why he hadn't given me a gown or a towel or something. He came back in and asked me to lay down on the bed. I remember feeling so vulnerable in front of this man as I lay there in my underwear as he proceeded to manipulate my body. The anxiety I felt was made worse by the fact that due to my hearing loss and him having a soft quiet voice I couldn't hear what he was saying. I just thought whatever he did could only prove to be beneficial so said yes to everything he asked. I could hear the cracking sound (it's normal) as he manipulated my spine into place but it didn't bother me. Manipulation of my leg had a positive result in reducing my hip pain. When I got home, I searched on the Internet to find out if it was usual for Osteomyologists to see you in your underwear and it was, so even though I found it a bit strange I was relieved about that. My husband and I read the reviews and found a positive one from a lady we knew so I contacted her and she suggested I go in some leggings and maybe a t-shirt next time. Sometimes the simple solutions are things we don't always think of for ourselves. As the saying goes, 'Two brains are always better than one.'

After my third appointment I didn't go back as I had started to notice a little whooshing sort of a noise similar to the sound of the wind which seemed to come from inside my right ear. It was so intrusive and frightening that it was difficult concentrating at work, especially when making phone calls. I was hoping it was just caused by something simple like ear wax but I'd heard of tinnitus (noise in the ears) that I'd suffered from intermittently in the past before getting my hearing aids.

I contacted the doctors who after looking in my ear was unable to find anything so referred me to Ear, Nose and Throat department at the hospital. The noise kept slowly increasingly getting louder until it felt as if it couldn't possibly get any louder. I started googling 'Tinnitus', accessing tinnitus groups on social media and phoning The British Tinnitus Association. It had reached a point where it was so loud that it was impossible to sleep. It became louder and faster each time I bent my neck in any way.

I remember going to work with my sick note and mentioning to my manager that I was aware one can get psychosis if they can't sleep. Psychosis is where you think things are happening that aren't a reality. It all became a bit of a blur from that point on but I remember becoming extremely anxious which caused a lack of appetite and weight loss. I was having regular appointments at the doctor's and received a letter saying I was malnourished.

My husband was desperately trying to help me as were my parents. My husband took time off work as he was also sleep deprived from trying to keep an eye on me. I kept wondering how I was ever going to live with that level of noise in my head, as I was thinking it couldn't get any louder. I was grieving for the peace in my head that was only a distant memory. I was all over the house with a duvet in a desperate attempt to get some sleep which didn't happen and left me extremely exhausted.

I started to feel very strange in my mind as if I'd taken some drugs and remember wondering if my husband had put anything in my food. He researched how to cure tinnitus and brought me apple cider vinegar to drink every morning in an attempt to cure me of it. I became very suspicious as it tasted so awful and I was beginning to feel strange as if I'd taken some drugs. It made me wonder if he was putting something in it so I was tipping it down the sink when he wasn't looking. I became very paranoid and I apparently said I wondered if he was trying to poison me. Those type of thoughts are common with psychosis.

I remember pacing the house whilst scrunching my hair as the anxiety was going through the roof. I was tried on several medications that didn't suite me for one reason or another but was then prescribed something called mirtazapine that was for appetite as well as anxiety and depression. My parents were visiting regularly. The doctor told me she was worried about me and said to me, "people with tinnitus have taken their own lives because it can be too distressing for them and we aren't going to let that happen to you". I remember feeling suicidal and just wanting to end my life and was thinking about every possible way I could achieve it. However, thoughts were going through my head about whether I would still end up in heaven as I was aware that life should be solely God's decision to end. I sure didn't want to be in the hell that the Bible describes as being a lake of fire. However, it was proving to be impossible to live with that level of torment in my head so I tried to leave the house with all the medication I had, but my husband was keeping a close eye on me.

Then I did something I never thought I would ever do and that was to try to end my own life. Thanks to my husband for intervening, it didn't end as badly as it could have done. When I was on the road to recovery, I read the leaflet from the antidepressants I'd been prescribed and was shocked to discover that they can enhance suicidal thoughts when it's initially taken. I couldn't understand why the GP would fail to mention something as important as that to me. Yet she was otherwise very good. She mentioned that the tinnitus had caused a mental health problem.

At the same time, I also remember wondering why God would allow someone to reach a point where they actually don't want to live anymore. Then it dawned on me that there is such a thing as a 'suicidal spirit' which it one of the evil spirits. Evil spirits enter us when we are vulnerable, for example by my not being able to sleep or when we are outside of God's covering by sinning for example. I had also expressed my wish to die rather than live with the tinnitus, so with that kind of negative talk we are unconsciously inviting evil spirits in. We can say negative things over ourselves unconsciously and are in effect cursing ourselves. As I've explained elsewhere, we don't realise how much power there actually is in the tongue. *'There is the power of life and death in the tongue' (Proverbs18:21).* There is also a 'spirit of death' that causes us to believe that life is hopeless and without meaning and brings with it an inclination to focus on death. Evil spirits are a subject I don't think we will ever fully understand.

One well known Christian who told me, 'God won't give you more than you can bear' proved to be wrong in my case. I think that often people misinterpret the scripture, *'And God is faithful; he will not let you be tempted beyond what you can bear'. (1 Corinthians 10:13).*

That morning my parents arrived and took me to stay with them overnight as I had a dentist's appointment the next day to remove a tooth. I remember telling them I couldn't go as having a tooth removed is one thing that causes me anxiety and I was already very anxious. They informed me I had to go, so they proceeded to drive me there but could see how unwell I was so they took me to the doctor instead. I remember sitting with the GP and the next thing I knew I was surrounded by lots of people. I recognised one as being a CPN (community pychiatric nurse) who had worked with me supporting a client who I supported in my line of work as a support worker. I remember being asked what I feared most about going to hospital and I'd told them it was seeing my work colleagues. My colleagues visited the psychiatric hospital as part of their job. Thankfully they were stopped from visiting the ward whilst I was there. I asked if I could go home to collect some belongings but was told I had to write a list for my husband to do that. I was informed I was being sectioned under the Mental Health Act for a twenty-eight-day assessment to be diagnosed. I later learnt that a Social Worker who was present was one I'd spoken to several times on the phone regarding a client I supported. That's what made it more distressing because it meant that now I was on the other side so to speak. I was the one needing support in the same way as many of the clients did whom I'd supported over the years. It increased the distress I was feeling of not only being so very unwell but of my stay in hospital in a locked ward. I was where many of the people I'd supported had been and feared going again. My fear was huge, but fear of what I wasn't quite sure. Fear of the unknown and of not being in control I suppose, of not being in control of my mind as was the case. In fact, it was terrifying, traumatic, extremely distressing and overwhelming. It felt as if I was in a dream, or had taken some illegal drugs.

Upon arrival all baggage was checked for anything you shouldn't have or could harm yourself with. Belts, shoe laces and mobile phone chargers were confiscated. The first two weeks were very much a blur like being in a dream, I only remember snippets of what happened. I remember singing every time a girl called Lucy walked past me, I sang the Beetles song 'Lucy in the sky with Diamonds'. People looked surreal. I didn't want to be there, I hated it. I couldn't believe there were people who actually liked being in there. There were patients who were regulars, for them it was like a revolving door. I never wanted it to be like that for me. I was unable to process my thoughts. I kept pacing up and down the corridors scrunching my hair due to my distress and anxiety, which was heightened by being in there. One patient asked if I had nits. I found it a struggle to sit down for more than a short time. I had hot flushes.

I was put on some medication that increased my appetite a lot. It was one of the side effects but benefitted my weight. My parents were bringing food to help me gain the weight I'd lost, so I ate sandwiches, crisps, bananas and desserts after eating my lunch. The first time I was allowed to leave the hospital after the four weeks I went to the shop with another patient where I bought £14 worth of food including a tin of mackerel, sandwiches, wraps, chocolate and a bread loaf, some of which I didn't eat. I only knew I'd bought them when I found the receipt days later. It was totally out of character for me.

The maintenance men were full of tattoos which scared me. There are some lovely tattoos but lots of tattoos, I've noticed, are of evil things such as faces of demons. Thankfully I've never been interested in wanting a tattoo, as God said, *'Do not cut your bodies for the dead, and do not mark your skin with tattoos. I am the Lord' (Leviticus 19:28).* Also, because God talks about our bodies as being a Temple of the living God it wouldn't seem right to mark it in that way.

I was afraid of being there and what was going to happen next. My blood pressure, pulse and temperature were taken daily. They monitored everything I ate and I was weighed regularly. There were no set appointments. People such as the Psychiatrist just called people in to see him at random. I struggled to speak to him as I was unable to process my thoughts but also because I was paranoid and very mistrustful. I didn't want to admit to anyone that I was struggling to function, or even to get in the shower as I wasn't able to accept that I'd lost my independence. It felt totally degrading. But throughout the whole of my breakdown God enabled me to maintain my wisdom and discernment. I didn't feel a peace about speaking to staff at hospital about my Christianity.

I've later heard several people with mental health problems say that their Christianity has been put down to part of their mental illness by mental health professionals. Then the danger is that people are medicated for what is just their faith. That's what I was trying to avoid.

I felt paranoid, as well as mistrusting, but still seemed to have a certain amount of wisdom about me. The only people I was able to fully trust were my parents and sister. I should explain that I was intolerant to wheat and dairy products, and had to follow a wheat free and dairy free diet. I began to suspect that the staff were asking them to test me by bringing the foods I was intolerant to, to test whether I was telling the truth.

During visiting hours, we often sat in the dining room and I could hear staff preparing things ready for tea behind the closed hatch doors and I thought they were trying to listen into our conversation so that they could report back to the nurses. When I mentioned this to one of my CPNs, at a much later date, he said, 'you weren't probably wrong there'. I replied 'so I wasn't that mad then!'. I had many visitors but even though I wanted to see people I didn't at the same time, if that makes sense, because I didn't like people seeing me so unwell. I felt embarrassed and ashamed. My friend Penny visited with her husband Iain and brought me this beautiful poem she wrote for me inspired by God.

Julie You are Special
A child of God most high
He made you in his image
You're the apple of his eye

Julie, God is pouring out
His precious love on you
Don't forget how much he cares
You're in his chosen few

He wants to paint a big bright smile
Upon your face today
And says walk in my light my child
As I light up the way

He had a perfect plan for you
Of hope of joy and peace
Just let his love pour in your heart
This battle soon will cease

Julie, know you're loved so much
God has a need of you
You are unique unto the Lord
His blessings make you new

Jesus says come unto me
And rest a little while
Just let me hold you in my arms
My very precious child

Just let him take your sorrows
And turn them into light
He says together we will sour

Each battle we will fight

So, Julie, know you're special
Unto the Lord most high
He has a perfect plan for you
On eagle's wings you'll fly

(By Penny Martin 2019)

I had my Bible with me but struggled to read any
and had a radio but struggled to listen to that either.
I felt totally disconnected from the God who loved
me.

Extremely loud buzzers went off and many staff ran
to help on which ever ward it had occurred.
Thankfully I was placed on the women only ward,
as I felt more comfortable with that than the thought
of being with any male patients. We had no choice
but to drink from plastic mugs that were either dark
blue or pillar box red as were told we couldn't have
ceramic ones due to patients throwing and breaking
them. Patient meetings took place every evening
where things like that were discussed. Someone
mentioned that we could catch something from the
mugs due to us sharing them especially if they
weren't washed properly. We made our own hot
drinks in a little kitchen and I caught certain
patients drinking straight from the bottle of milk.
Yuck, that's what we had to endure.

We had to queue up for medication that was

distributed in the clinic. I would check what they were giving me and asked to see the boxes. I often noticed a change in colour, shape or amount. They told me it was because they'd ran out of for example the 100mg so had to give me two 50mg or was sometimes due to different branding. Once there was a totally different tablet (an antipsychotic) the Psychiatrist had prescribed but hadn't told me about. For that reason, I didn't want to take it. I was very angry about it so I refused to take it. But they locked me in the clinic and told me I'd be given an injection if I didn't. Since then, they asked me to open my mouth to check if I'd swallowed it.

A Psychiatric Nurse was on the ward as an inpatient which made me think she was there undercover to help diagnose me. Maybe I was right, I don't know. There appeared to be nothing wrong with most of the patients. However, mental illness is something you can't see. It's classed as an invisible illness. While supporting people with mental illness I often thought I wish I could just get inside their head so I could understand what they were experiencing. Some of the hospital patients became aggressive, needing to be restrained. I found this to be a frightening experience when I wasn't well. One young girl climbed on to the roof outside and damaged her foot. Its beyond me how she managed it. Another patient escaped out the front door and ran off. I felt like escaping but knew there was no point because I'd only have to go back. I think the police brought her back.

I was told I'd been diagnosed with anxiety and depression and later was informed I was being placed with the Psychosis team (mental health team for support after discharge) but not to dwell on the psychosis bit too much. Then one of my sick notes had 'psychosis and depression' written on it. Psychosis can be common with severe depression.

I was in hospital for seven weeks in total, getting some home leave after four weeks. I remember going out on leave one afternoon for lunch with my mum and sister. Whilst in the pub I don't know what overtook me but all I remember was seeing a pizza (which is something I don't usually eat) on the counter and a having a strong compulsion that caused me to go and take a piece and eat it. That was totally out of character for me and it isn't the done thing. It was a pizza that had been waiting to be served to a customer. As you can imagine it was most embarrassing for my poor Mum who was apologising and offering to pay for it. My sister missed the whole experience (lucky for her) as she was parking her car. It's most awful how our minds can wrongly operate. Later my mum told me the chef was annoyed and had told us to just get out. Thankfully we were able to laugh about it when I was well.

After being discharged from hospital, I was still very unwell, extremely anxious, feeling suicidal on a daily basis, every morning wishing I hadn't woken up. The psychotic symptoms disappeared even after I stopped taking the medication but I was taking the highest dose of mirtazapine (an antidepressant). I dreaded the day ahead which was so long and boring as I was unable to find interest in any of my hobbies or anything else for that matter. I found it such a struggle to get out of bed feeling as if something was pinning me down. Many of the days I was unable to shower or dress. I was unable to read or concentrate on anything or even to cook at first. Even the simplest of decisions was impossible. Everything was such a chore and often impossible to achieve. My mum wanted me to go and stay with her so she could care for me but the thought of any change terrified me as it felt too traumatic to endure. Home was my safe place if you like, even though I didn't really always feel safe. I just wandered from the house to the garden and back.

It was an impossibility at times just to move from the bed or chair to answer the phone. It's difficult to explain to anyone. I remember my sister once phoning and sounding annoyed asking, 'what's happening? I've been trying to get hold of you'. But I didn't know how to explain why I couldn't do it. My husband didn't like answering the phone because he didn't know what to say to family or people if they asked him questions. He doesn't cope with questions very well, he never has. It seems to feel too overwhelming for him. He deals with things in his own way by suppressing emotions, like a typical man going into his cave. I can't imagine how difficult my being unwell must have been for him. The most important thing now is that he stood by me.

I was even unable to pray and didn't quite know why. It was just that depression causes you to lose interest in the things you once enjoyed. However, I managed a little prayer just to ask God to bring me the right support. I questioned God as he'd healed me from 'social anxiety' several years earlier and I kept wondering why he'd allowed me to experience it again but ten times worse this time. I almost lost my faith and was just clinging on to God by my fingernails. 'Where had my faith gone?', I wondered. I was scared that it would never come back. Was it gone forever? The strong faith I'd developed over nineteen years, the faith I loved, the God I loved. Why was He allowing me to go through this terrible, horrendous ordeal? I felt so cut off from God. That in itself is a horrible place to be. I needed others to have the faith for me that I couldn't have. My love and faithfulness to God was being tested and it's a difficult test that many people fail to pass. Still loving God when He allows you to go through a horrendous situation is extremely tough. But this testing occurs so that we will have perseverance and our character grows as a result of it. *'Consider it pure joy, my brothers and sisters, whenever you face trials of many kinds, because you know that the testing of your faith produces perseverance' (James 1:2-3).*

Job was tested by God. The enemy told God that if he takes everything away from Job that he would curse God and die. God allowed it to happen and proved the enemy wrong. Job kept his faith.

Regarding the whole experience of my breakdown, I have since felt God saying to me "I can't bring a change in you if you don't allow the trials". '*Not only that, but we also rejoice in our sufferings, because we know that suffering produces perseverance; perseverance, character; and character, hope'. (Romans 5:3).*

It felt like one huge enemy attack. A quote I read said, 'God will allow you to go through places you don't understand, just to bring you to the place where He needs you to be.' I felt that place was a deeper faith but also a deeper understanding of those with mental health problems and suicidal thoughts.

Although at times it felt like God had abandoned me, I knew He was there with me because scripture said so. It was the only thing I had left to cling to. *Psalm 34:18 says, 'the Lord is close to the broken-hearted; he rescues those whose spirits are crushed'. 'For God has said, "I will never fail you. I will never abandon you". (Hebrews 13:5).* It's reassuring to know that God is always with us, He will never leave us. His Spirit lives inside us. God's promises are true even when we don't feel they are. We need to stand on the truth and not doubt His Word.

As I am a sensitive, empathic person the numb feeling I then had, not being able to cry or express any emotion, felt alien to me. I wanted to cry and let all the pent-up emotions out but nothing was coming forth. I was only sleeping three to four hours each night. My family and husband were desperately wanting to help but felt helpless and were forced to stand by and watch me as I seemed to deteriorate even further.

I started catastrophising (thinking of the worst outcome and believing it to be true). This further increased the anxiety I was feeling. I was thinking about losing my job, then having no income, then thinking my husband wouldn't want me because I wasn't getting better, that I would be homeless if we separated. All sorts of negative thoughts were going through my mind. I was distraught.

My mum who was a massive support by phoning me daily when she wasn't visiting, kept telling me that I would get through it and come out stronger. However, I was unable to see a way out. She said she wished she could do more to help but she did more than she will ever realise as those hour-long phone calls kept me alive, kept me going and gave me that ever so tiny glimmer of hope when I was unable to see any. Even if it was only the hope that there was someone out there who cared and loved me.

I attended a couple of outpatient appointments with the Psychiatrist. When she left, I was given an appointment with another lady whom I recognised straight away and she recognised me. When she told me she knew me from somewhere I told her it was from work as she had supported one of my clients. I was pleased by that as I knew she was good at her job and I was blessed to have her as my Nurse Practitioner. I was able to explain all my symptoms to her including major memory problems, those of fear that something bad was going to happen and of not being able to get certain things out of my mind such as past clients who had died and memories of the worst clients, I'd worked with even years ago. She explained I was suffering severe depression. I remember bursting into tears (yes, I cried for the first time in what seemed like an eternity) and said, 'no wonder I've been struggling so much then.'

Nine months after being discharged from hospital I still wasn't making any improvement. I hardly went out of the house, my confidence and self-esteem were low, which the CPN (community psychiatric nurse) said was normal when people have been in hospital, especially when it was their first admission and with people who were high functioning like me. The odd times I did manage to go out I felt so distressed because I was unable to function as I had before being ill so it caused even more distress and anxiety. The whole experience was terrifying! I just wanted some normality back in my life.

Tinnitus

My referral to the Ear, Nose and Throat department at the hospital confirmed that the whooshing noise I experienced as a result of the Ostemyologists manipulation was tinnitus. A definition by McFadden stated 'tinnitus is the unconscious expression of a sound that originates in an involuntary manner in the head if its owner.' Sounds can be anything ranging from whooshing, buzzing, humming, hissing, whistling to name a few and can contain a mixture of any. Volume levels can fluctuate and often increase due to stress, tiredness, ill health or worsening of health. One in eight people in the UK experience persistent tinnitus.

Because there isn't any treatment for tinnitus, I was referred to a management group for a couple of hours where we were informed about different coping mechanisms. The key is to distract yourself so you aren't focusing on the noise and to use music as background noise. My hearing aids help as they amplify external sounds that mask the tinnitus a little. Given time, mine became manageable on its own, thank goodness. What happens after some time is that you habituate to the new sound, which means that your brain becomes accustomed to it and you become less aware of the noise. People often say they notice their tinnitus when they go to bed and that's because they are in a quiet room so they are focused on it more. It's like if you sit in a quiet room doing nothing with a ticking clock you hear that clock because you will focus on it and the more you focus on it the louder it can appear to sound.

Mine reacts to my bending my head or neck. Therefore, if I move my head or neck or go to the toilet, would you believe, the whooshing sound becomes louder and faster. I read up about tinnitus and something I wasn't aware of is that there are different types. Certain types similar to my sound can be related to blood flow. Someone said that bending your neck puts pressure on blood vessels and arteries.

I read an interesting article about Elvis Presley's death when I researched it for a substance misuse course I was doing. He apparently died on the toilet of a heart attack due to constipation putting strain on his heart. This made me think about the tinnitus I have as arteries and blood vessels are connected to the heart. I'm don't mean I think I'm going to die in the same way or have a heart attack.

Another challenge I experience that can commonly occur with tinnitus is noise sensitivity (hyperacusis). Many people with autism also struggle with this. Certain noises appear too loud for the brain to handle. At the tinnitus group we were told about a guy who couldn't stand the sound of his wife eating crisps but it doesn't bother him when the dog eats crisps. I told them that the noise I struggle with is my husband's voice. They all started laughing. I told them that thankfully with volume control on hearing aids I can turn him down.

Menopause and Medication Withdrawal

Just to complicate matters, a year after the start of my breakdown the doctors established that I was probably going through the menopause, which presented me with new challenges.

I've talked to several other women who were experiencing menopausal symptoms and confirmed that mood swings, fatigue and muscle aches are some of the symptoms. Basically, their moods are up and down and they can start struggling with depression. One in ten women may encounter depression during this time. They are more likely to develop depression during this time if they have had a depressive episode in the past. However, my depression wasn't a symptom of menopause which I will explain later.

I could often sleep for ten hours and still feel fatigue. I can feel like my power is running on low or almost empty, like my get up and go has diminished. The best way of describing my symptoms is that they are not too unlike how you can feel when you have the flu or a virus.

One of the nurses at the doctor's surgery said, 'The joys of being a woman! There are none!', which I found quite funny.

I was talking to my male Community Psychiatric Nurse (CPN) and I said I'm feeling better now as last time he visited I'd been suffering with a low mood for a week. I said, "It must be the menopause because often I can't see a reason for it". He said, "We can often underestimate the menopause can't we! We can think all it is, is a few hot flushes and that's it. All I can say is, I'm glad I'm a man". So, for all you men out there, just be glad you are a man.

I've found the doctors to be unsupportive with the menopause in discussing symptoms or offering any options for treatment. I've heard that to be other women's experiences too.

I could feel I was doing well then all of a sudden got a few really down days. I've suffered from lack of energy, and tiring easily for most of my life and muscle aches for years; symptoms I'd just put down to my underactive thyroid but had worked it out a couple of years ago that I could have fibromyalgia.

However, I remember saying to both of my CPNs that I didn't feel this fatigued when I was on the higher dose of mirtazapine (antidepressant). They both said they didn't think it was anything to do with the medication as it's more sedating at lower doses. I was offered to increase the dose again but managed to get through it without. It turned out that even though I was in menopause some of the symptoms were related to reduction in medication (withdrawal symptoms) which explained why I wasn't as fatigued on the higher dose and some to what I'd thought for a long time, fibromyalgia.

My CPN informed me I could reduce my medication again as I'd been on it over one year and by September 2020, I was doing so well mentally that he signed me off from their team and back to primary (GP) care. In October of 2020 I decided to try reducing my medication but a week later I began experiencing severe withdrawal symptoms. These included vomiting, cold shivers, intense full body muscle aches, hot flushes, reduced appetite, bad headaches and extreme severe fatigue. I felt as if I had a severe dose of food poisoning and the doctors could do nothing to help me. I wasn't prepared for it at all.

That's when it dawned on me that was the reason, I was severely fatigued and depressed during lockdown when I reduced from the highest dose previously. I was amazed the mental health nurses weren't aware of it. Withdrawal symptoms can also include depression and anxiety during withdrawal can cause people to feel it's a return of their mental health symptoms when that isn't always the case. Several people who were prescribed mirtazapine for insomnia have experienced depression during withdrawal and were people who'd never suffered depression before.

I found a very informative and supportive Facebook group where others were also finding it to be an ordeal to come off, so have needed to taper slowly by making a liquid of the pills and measuring it in a syringe. I started doing this but it wasn't ideal. The

GP gave me bad advice by telling me to skip doses. I read evidence that missing doses increased withdrawal symptoms. It took for me to write to the GP practice manager before I was prescribed the liquid in order to taper gradually.

God gave me the strength to endure the challenging seventeen months taper.

Fibromyalgia

As my physical health symptoms were taking a turn for the worst during lockdown, I asked the doctor to refer me to see if I had fibromyalgia. He took bloods and, as nothing showed up, referred me to rheumatology.

My appointment was in September 2020. The Consultant read the list of my symptoms that I had taken with me, examined me and informed me that I had fibromyalgia. I got told it wasn't life threatening, was given an information booklet and told I'd be referred for Physiotherapy. Surprisingly the Consultant informed me there are medications you can take for it but he doesn't believe they work. My thoughts were that he must never have experienced severe pain because if you are in that amount of pain, you need something. I later found out that fibromyalgia doesn't respond well to pain medication but sometimes just having something to take the edge off helps. I asked the Consultant if my breakdown last year could have contributed to the symptoms worsening. When I asked, he confirmed with me that psychological factors such as that can make fibromyalgia worse.

According to Fibromyalgia UK 2 per cent of the population are diagnosed with fibromyalgia. It's a condition that affects many more women than men. Research has found that that people suffering from fibromyalgia are 4.5 times more likely to have hearing loss than people who don't have the illness.

It's characterised by chronic widespread pain, chronic fatigue, stiffness, headaches, IBS, stiffness after sitting or sleeping, sleep that doesn't leave you refreshed amongst numerous other symptoms. Body temperature isn't regulated as it should be. Symptoms are unpredictable as they can fluctuate by the day or hour. Overall, it's a debilitating and incapacitating condition.

When you say fatigue or even fatigue, I don't think people get it. Fatigue is unlike usual tiredness. It's a constant lack of energy. I can feel absolutely drained to the point of exhaustion. Exhaustion can hit as quick as the flick of a light switch. Pain can also drain energy. When fatigue is at its worst my speech can been slurred. If people didn't know me, they could think I've taken some drugs or been drinking.

Fibromyalgia also causes people to experience what is termed as 'brain fog'. It's having difficulty with cognition or mental clarity and memory loss. I've explained brain fog in that I can't think straight. I can lack concentration for example if I'm making a cup of tea when the phone rings, I can forget I was making the cup of tea. I can be distracted easily and have become an expert in cleaning burnt pans. Another hazard is leaving the cooker ring on after I've finished cooking. Sometimes I can forget what I'm about to say in the middles of a sentence or what I was just about to tell someone suddenly disappears from my mind.

There are some advantages to having memory problems such as when I watch a film for the second time it can be as if I've watched it for the first time. I can't think of any others right now but I'm sure there are some. I always try to look on the bright side. The Monty Python song has just come to mind, 'Look on the bright side of life.'

'Post exertional malaise' is when symptoms worsen due to minor physical or mental exertion. This can last for one to three days or even weeks. Sufferers call it a 'crash' due to the crashing of energy. I say, "my battery has gone flat" as I've exceeded my energy limit and reached exhaustion. It could be a similar effect to what people experience after they have run a 10k marathon. An example of post exertional malaise was when we went to Estonia.

During a mission trip to Estonia for a week, myself and my husband were asked to be on the door welcoming people in. We were expected to be there morning and evening. In the middle of the week, I woke up one day completely exhausted and being unable to lift myself out of bed. Consequently, I had to spend the full day resting until I regained some energy. I now take ginseng if I know I'm going to be doing something that will use more energy. It helps!

'The Spoon Theory' can be a useful tool to explain to others how our chronic illness or limited energy affects us. It's a theory that a spoon is a unit of energy. People with fibromyalgia have limited energy. It may take someone one spoon to get dressed but two spoons to have a shower for example. We need to think carefully how we are going to use our energy each day because when the spoons have been used our energy has run out. I've heard it said when you have a chronic illness that causes fatigue to think of your energy like money. Such a simple analogy (if that's the correct terminology) to help others understand.

My pain is similar to a flu-like ache in muscles and joints. Fibromyalgia UK states that fibromyalgia pain can be more painful than arthritis. Pain levels can be very severe that they can even prevent one from being able to function. I can often feel as if I've woken with a hangover as I wake up feeling tired and rough, even after a good night's sleep. That is supposedly due to not getting the deep sleep that refreshes us. Someone described fibromyalgia as feeling like they have jet lag. Jet lag, flu or hangover are the best ways of describing it to those who don't have it.

'Gulf War Syndrome' affected veterans of the Persian Gulf War 1990-1991. Symptoms were similar to fibromyalgia including fatigue, cognitive problems, insomnia, rashes, muscle pain and diarrhoea. Likely causes were chemicals including chemical warfare and psychological factors.

When I entered the menopause, I discovered that the change in my hormones caused my existing symptoms to flare. A 'flare' means worsening of symptoms and can happen at any time for various reasons or for no reason at all. It's a temporary setback that can last anytime from days to weeks or even months. Once the menopause hit, I found I was no longer physically well enough to work. Many people with fibromyalgia have found symptoms to worsen around menstruation and as well as with age.

I read that with fibromyalgia our body is permanently in the stress response mode. Therefore, muscles are tight and energy is being used up as it is directed to the muscles. Reasons for fibromyalgia aren't fully understood but it often occurs after trauma or glandular fever and I've experienced both. I also read that more often than not there is an imbalance in the stress coping hormones.

There is no current cure and it can be challenging to manage symptoms. I've learnt to pace myself which means doing an activity then resting throughout the day and breaking activities into smaller manageable tasks. I try to listen to my body so if I need to rest, I try to rest. On days when I have more energy if I do more, I've learnt I can suffer for it for a day or two afterwards. When we've lived with a symptom for a long time, we can learn our own ways of coping. For example, to cope with memory loss I do the following:

- I write everything down within different notebooks and lists.
- I write to do lists
- Put reminders on my mobile as well as in my diary of activities/ groups I take part in on a weekly basis.

For pain management I use an electric heat pad, tens machine, hot water bottle, stress management and exercise. The Pilates class I attended for several years proved to beneficial but a reduction in energy meant I was forced to give it up. Movement is good as sitting too much tends to cause more muscle tension. The Physiotherapist referred me to some gym session lead by a Physiotherapist. I told him I'd give it a go but I didn't think I'd be able to do it. I just did what I could but was amazed at how much looser I was even after one session.

Getting the diagnosis was a somewhat emotional experience but also a relief to finally have a name for what I'd been experiencing all these years. It took the pressure off me from feeling that I had to try and function like a healthy person. I'm relieved I no longer have the pressure of having to go to work (since losing my job) when I'm feeling fatigued or in too much pain. It's easier to accept my struggles now I have a reason for them.

Since the diagnosis everything I'd struggled with started making sense. For instance, I realised why I struggled to remember where I'd parked the car at the supermarket. I had a reason for the years of ongoing backache I'd put down a result of all the lifting I did when working in the Nursing Home.

I attended the fibromyalgia support group in Darlington and loved it. It was great to just chat and socialise with others who could understand. Facebook groups again have been where I've learnt so much from others with fibromyalgia. I've learnt that everyone is different, everyone's pain is different and symptoms vary. I used to think fibromyalgia was only about muscle pain but learnt it's so much more than that. It might seem like there is a lot wrong with us but it's a condition with numerous symptoms. I've learnt over the years that Pilates has always helped me and that's because those tight tense muscles in my body are getting stretched out. Therefore, it makes me more flexible.

Most of the time I just want people to validate my struggles, how I'm feeling, not try to minimise them or encourage me to be any different. However, I don't reject a little advice. For someone to say, 'I get that', or 'I hear you' or 'I understand' can go a long way to making me feel better emotionally.

I find that when I didn't have a diagnosis often people would dispute how I am and say 'Oh you can do it'. However, we are the best ones to know the limitations of our own bodies. Pushing your body when it's telling you to rest doesn't do it any good. It can just mean that you will feel worse for it, then that only leads to more stress, more negative emotions, frustration, anger etc.

It can be one of the hardest things to accept that you have a chronic illness because for me it would be nice to still be able to still do what others can do, attend Zumba, walk for miles, climb hills, go skiing. But I have no choice but to accept my limitations and miss out on certain things. It doesn't bother me anymore as I've accomplished things and had an interesting life. People can go through a grieving process and grieve the loss of the person they used to be. It takes time to come to terms with the new you who can be very different from the person you previously were. I'm just so thankful to God for what I can do and I focus on those rather than on what I can't do. I can walk (even if I'm slow sometimes), I get out and mix with people, I'm able to prepare and cook tea and do housework even if I have to pace myself and only do a little each day. With chronic illness you have to learn to accept the unpredictability and can't always plan too much. One day I might feel reasonably ok, the next I may not be able to do anything but rest all day and another I may be in too much pain. Coping with chronic illness is all about learning to listen to your body, learning the balance between fighting and surrendering and praying for God to give you strength and grace to get through it. What helps is that I've always been a resilient, optimistic person. I can laugh at myself and the ability to do so goes a long way. But there are times when I just get tired of being sick and tired.

Lockdown

Only a year after the start of my breakdown, just as I was enjoying getting out and about a couple of months later, we found ourselves in some very strange times when the Coronavirus (COVID-19) hit. Many people were dying and many were treated in hospital and needing to be on ventilators to enable them to breathe. Boris Johnson the Prime Minister caught the virus and was hospitalised. But it came to light that the Doctor who was treating him was a Christian so I prayed that he would have a chance to share the gospel with him.

The NHS wasn't prepared for this massive crisis, but they were doing an amazing job. As the virus was highly contagious, we went into Government lead 'lockdown' where the country almost came to a standstill. 'Lockdown' was a term to describe a period where everyone who could had to remain at home and only go out for essentials. People worked from home if they could and shops, pubs, clubs, cafes, hairdressers and churches were forced to close. We were only permitted to go out once a day for exercise and for essentials as shops that sold food and chemists were the only places open.

It was thought that the virus could be spread via breath and by touching contaminated items so we were advised to wash our hands for twenty seconds after being outside. Shopping and the post could be contaminated so we were advised to leave it out for two days until the germs had disappeared. During this time businesses went into liquidation and many people were made redundant. It was a time where mental health problems and domestic abuse were on the rise. It was a time where families were forced together for good or bad. As far as it was possible GP and hospital appointments were carried out over the phone and still are.

We came out of lockdown to only be back in a similar place a couple of months later as death rates rose again. This occurred three times in total. It came into effect that everyone had to wear masks whilst in shops, hairdressers etc. Shops also had plastic screens at checkouts. This presented new challenges for those with hearing loss and especially those needing to lip read. I find it stressful and draining when I'm not hearing what people are saying and having to ask them to repeat then sometimes still not hearing all that they've said.

People stocked up on perishable items and toilet rolls which meant that many people struggled to find these items as shops were sold out. It was strange seeing shop shelves totally bare. To be honest all this behaviour was motivated by fear of not having enough including becoming ill and not being able to get to the shops to buy those items.

It would have been so easy to allow my thoughts to run away with me and let my mind be consumed with the fear of it all, as so many people were. Especially when I was in the early stages of recovery from my breakdown and withdrawing from a reduction in the antidepressants. The scripture comes to mind in Matthew 6:34 *'So don't worry about tomorrow, for tomorrow will bring its own worries. Today's trouble is enough for today'.* I did my best to keep focused on God and take one day at a time limiting what information I allowed into my mind by not watching the news or reading newspapers. I just subscribed to Coronavirus update via e-mail where I could choose what to read or not to read it at all. All sorts of conspiracy theories were going round but I chose to remember that God is all powerful and above everything and that he always knows what He is doing. His ways are higher than ours as he sees the bigger picture when we only see situations in part.

But it was a time where God was shaping His Kingdom. We had more time to spend with God praying and reading His Word. It forced Christians to be creative about new ways to share the gospel and how to do church. I got some thank you cards with the gospel on the back that I gave to shop workers who served me and bus drivers. I posted some Easter cards with Christian Easter poems in written by my friend Penny. I have a video of me sharing my healing from major depression, so I shared that on a couple of groups including the Tinnitus Success Stories group and Christians with Depression and Anxiety group on Facebook to give people hope.

The situation caused churches to start thinking about being creative therefore many conducted services online. This meant they were accessible to different people groups. When people were allowed to go out more, a Drive in Church operated for one month in Darlington. It was interesting as people tooted their horns when they would normally clap. Drive in cinemas then opened. When churches could open again, they did with measures in place such as distancing between seats and no singing. It became compulsory to wear face masks on public transport and in shops. This made it more difficult for the hearing impaired like myself. All shops have hand sanitiser at the door as you go in. There were restrictions on the amount of people they were letting into a shop at one time which meant that often people had to queue to go shopping. We went to a furniture shop where our temperature was taken upon entering and they had disposable pens.

When lockdown initially occurred, I was low in mood but then I adapted to it and things got easier. It was an extremely frightening time for many people as it was a very new experience. I began to see the benefits of not having the pressure of having to attend appointments and having more time to spend with God. I was forced to slow down which was a good thing considering I don't have a lot of energy.

I kept my brain thinking and active by working through Distance Learning courses online. I dug my cross stitch out of the loft which I hadn't done for years and made a couple of book marks and coasters for friends' birthdays. I also tried to reach out to others who I knew in the area who were over the age of seventy. This is one of the activities listed in the 5 Steps to Wellbeing described on the NHS website.

I started listening to 'Power Hour' teaching by a group of Prophets online four days a week which kept me grounded and gave me something to look forward to. Thursday nights Celebrate Recovery moved to zoom, an online platform where we met to watch the video then discuss the questions in groups just as we did when we met in person. It provided that little bit of contact with others. It's a Christ centred course adapted from the twelve steps to recovery that addicts follow in their group meetings. The main thing I took away from it was that God isn't always enough. We need to share our struggles with others by talking and praying together. Attending courses online meant that I could hear what everyone was saying whereas when I've attended them in person in a group, I would ensure I'd arrive early so I could sit near the speaker but then miss what other participants would say. Group work would also pose a challenge as I would hear the chatter of others talking in their groups preventing me from hearing what some of the people in my group were saying.

Relationship Difficulties

As I've said 'Celebrate Recovery' taught me the importance, and often necessity at times of talking with others as well as God. It was common practice for me not to share with anyone about the difficulties in my marriage (all marriages have them) as I did not want to put my husband down. I took the scripture '*Do not let any unwholesome talk come out of your mouths, but only what is helpful for building others up according to their needs, that it may benefit those who listen*' in Ephesians 2:29, literally. It has only been in times of complete and utter desperation that I've reached out for support. There are times when I've prayed for someone to talk to, and God in His grace, has sent the right person to help me.

Now I will remind you that we believe God brought us together and He doesn't make mistakes. However, the enemy doesn't want Christian marriages to succeed and can do all in his power to break them up. Another thing to bear in mind is that witches do pray for Christian marriages to break up. I married a Russian man who was brought up under Communism and been in the Russian army amongst other challenges. He has a blunt and direct approach. During a recent conversation this year he mentioned that a certain person was a typical Russian. When I asked him what that was, he told me that they think they know best. I laughed as that's exactly what he is like. He informed me that Russians think we English people are blessed. He said that when they see us crying, they think it's not a big issue and we just need to man up and get on with it. This mindset is a result of Russians being brought up in a tough country, often living in poverty. When I visited Russia, I noticed that the majority of the people didn't smile. They didn't have any joy and I felt they needed Jesus in their lives. I thank God for David Hathaway who visited the country on many occasions to preach and share God's Word until the Russian government put a stop to it all.

Life experiences influence our characters and we can inherit certain personality traits from our parents. I will firstly add that my husband is a wonderful husband in many ways and is a wealth of fun. However, his often harsh, critical, authoritative approach and perfectionist style have brought me to my knees on many an occasion. It has caused intense pain in my heart, mind and soul, to the point of total distress that resulted in the need for inner healing. Healing released deep inner pain that had built up over the years. When your feelings aren't validated and you don't feel loved it can cause feelings of ongoing rejection. There were times when I longed for just an ounce of compassion, gentleness and tenderness but found myself being met with a harsh critical or authoritative word. It wasn't always what he said but the tone in which he said it. I just recently came to the realisation that he probably had a critical spirit in him.

My Church Home Group leader once told me something that made complete sense. She told me that what my husband isn't capable of giving me I will need to get from others. At times I've found compassionate people at groups or church and I feel we especially as women need this and need also to be compassionate to ourselves which I've learnt to do since my breakdown. I've had a tendency to be too hard on myself.

My friend used to remind me that he, my husband, has a hard exterior but a softness deep inside much like a hard-boiled sweet that has a soft centre. When we were at New Wine Christian Camp in August 2016, I went for prayer ministry and they got a vision for me of buttercup petals opening up petals to God's Life-giving warmth and love. They saw me reflecting the love of Jesus, that I'd received, back to my husband to break down those barriers and walls of hardness he'd developed around his heart. It is extremely encouraging when you are not seeing any change and God just speaks a word right into our heart. I felt empowered and uplifted by it. Over the next few years, I have continued to pray and very very gradually witnessed more and more of the softness of his heart coming through that hard exterior. God said '*I will give you a new heart and put a new spirit in you; I will remove from you your heart of stone and give you a heart of flesh*'.

(Ezekiel 36:26).

So those of you who are constantly praying for loved ones and not seeing any change, be encouraged as you don't know what God is doing inside them. It has been a long hard road and only those who have been in similar relationships seem to truly understand how difficult it is at times. I shared with another Christian who said her husband was similar and just simply said 'it's hard, it's hard'. That empathy of another person who understood was so comforting. Another lady was sharing about her husband who was similar and I suddenly started sobbing. It was one of those many inner healing encounters that I experienced. The lady said, 'that's resonating with you, isn't it?' Having those people there who could relate was such a relief and brought healing to my heart.

Searching

One of the disappointments I've been left to face, is when God hasn't healed me of something, I've asked Him to or been prayed for. Lack of healing has caused me to struggle with mixed emotions including frustration, hopelessness, lack of control and fear. Christianity can put pressure on you to be healed. Being told that God wants you well can be encouraging but can also make it impossible to accept your illness. It's difficult to accept ill health when you have Christians who tell you that you shouldn't accept it because it's not God's will for your life to be ill. Yet accepting it can ease the burden somewhat.

Physical healing in the Christian community is usually portrayed as being a touch from God resulting in an instant healing. This, often being the only focus for physical healing in churches, left me with questions and doubts, wondering if my lack of healing was maybe down to my having done something wrong. I was searching for answers by analysing myself. Was there any unconfessed sin in my life? Was I in any way not walking right with God? Was I not praying in the right way for God to heal me? Was there anyone I hadn't forgiven? I questioned whether I had enough faith to be healed, but realised that God said we only need faith the size of a mustard seed (*Luke 17:6*). I don't think it's all about faith, but belief. Not everyone believes they'll be healed.

Because I'd attended lots of prayer meetings over the years, yet hadn't experienced any physical healing for myself, it made it very difficult for me to believe that I would be healed. However, I often went forward for prayer in faith. I became tired of going out for prayer, wondering how long it would continue, but one thing I've never done is given up trying.

A friend's sister once pointed out to me that what we have to remember is that God isn't a slot machine. She went on to say that if He healed everyone who asked, then people would become Christians for that reason alone. It was a very valid point, adding what I believed at the time to be a final piece to my jigsaw of piecing things together.

However, Jesus wants us well. He took our sickness on the cross, *'But he was pierced for our transgressions, he was crushed for our iniquities; the punishment that brought us peace was on him, and by his wounds we are healed (Isaiah 53:5).'* I am now able to believe I am healed, but still waiting for it to manifest in my body. It's about resting in Jesus and what he has done for us on the cross. Physical symptoms of ill health can be a lie from the enemy. God doesn't want us to be sick, but unfortunately there is plenty of sickness out there.

I've witnessed and heard of many miracles of healings, which has always encouraged my faith. I remember God's faithfulness, how he has made a way for me in the past, enabling me to be free from sickness that I will mention later, giving me some hope for future healing.

I tried to figure it all out. I read numerous books and internet sites and did everything I could think of that I thought would help my healing to manifest itself. I got rid of everything I owned that I thought had anything to do with any dark spiritual attachment, including pictures I'd bought in Egypt /Israel, horror books, new age books, lucky charms and, lastly, my reflexology books. I didn't want to own anything that I felt could be hindering my healing.

At one point I thought that if God isn't going to heal me, I need to do something myself. I was so desperate to get well that I tried all sorts of different approaches such as homeopathy, bach flower remedies and other numerous supplements that claimed to improve the immune system but didn't seem to make any difference for me.

I also realised that in the race for finding ways to get better, I had not always made good decisions. For instance, I was persuaded by the staff at the Chinese medicine clinic, which I passed regularly, to go in for a chat. When I explained to them about my chemical sensitivity, I was told that if I took the pills, they could sell me, I'd be cured. I was so desperate at that point that I paid the £80 for one month supply of about 20 tiny pills per day. When I went back the next month to inform them that there was no change in my symptoms, they told me it was because I needed to take something else as well. I was skeptical and refused to spend any more money with them. I later learned it wasn't a good idea for Christians to get involved in alternative therapies and remedies due to the spiritual roots that may be involved.

The nutritionist who stated she was a gut specialist, diagnosed me with candida (yeast overgrowth). She placed me on a diet of no sugar, yeast or anything fermented, accompanied by supplements in an aim to kill off the candida. I was so desperate and determined to be free from my stomach pains that the diet didn't even prove to be much of a challenge.

After one year of being on the diet, tests confirmed I didn't have candida. But despite being told that this would cure my stomach pains, my symptoms were still the same.

I was then advised that there was a possibility I could have parasites. In faith I paid for the tests, which confirmed I did. I was informed that it could be the cause of my pains. I paid for the treatment even though there was no guarantee this would work. I finished the treatment to be left again without any change in my symptoms. I am very grateful that I had help with these issues, as it just shows what we can be dealing with in our bodies that we are unaware of. But my main aim was to be rid of my pain.

I later found out that 70 per cent of your immune system is in your gut. Therefore, if your good bacteria in your gut have reduced due to stress, taking antibiotics, etc., then your immune system will be weaker. As a result, we need probiotics to increase the good bacteria in our gut to improve our immune system. I realised then why all the supplements I'd taken hadn't seemed to help my immunity. When I started taking probiotics regularly, I didn't get the muscle pains and weakness to the same extent that I experienced for many years.

Sadly, my experience of the NHS has been more of a negative than a positive one, leaving me unable to trust what professionals tell me anymore. I understand that any health professional doesn't have all the answers. But at times my experience has been that doctors just find something to say to appease their patients, giving an answer that isn't necessarily the truth. I reached a point where I now question eve NHS professionals. The often desperate need for testing is overlooked due to lack of finances or having to keep within a budget. I'm not knocking the NHS, it's a blessing to have this service in the UK and I believe that God can and does use doctors but like everything else it does have its drawbacks.

The focus of the NHS is on preventing symptoms and not treating the cause, while this in the meantime can leave our health in a state of further decline and deterioration. This approach causes people to become dependent on prescription drugs. All medication has side effects, even if these aren't evident. Doctors then give out more medication to treat these side effects.

In my own strength

At times I've been trying to do things in my own strength rather than relying on and trusting in God.

The doctors were unable to help me with my IBS and MCS, just giving me painkillers or medication that didn't work or only worked for so long. Therefore, I was forced to take my health into my own hands by researching alternative healing online. Looking for answers can become an obsession. It can consume you and take over your life as it did for me at one point. So much time can be wasted due to our bodies being so complex and the conflicting information out there.

I became more and more confused, which partly contributed to a period of depression. Then I read in one of Joyce Meyer's books about why so many people are confused and God said to her; 'Tell them to stop trying to work everything out, and they will stop being confused.' It made perfect sense but wasn't easy to put into practice, as I am a person who naturally analyses everything. God said to Joyce: "Reasoning and confusion go together; you must lay aside carnal reasoning if you ever expect to have discernment." I'm not saying that researching is wrong but direction and discernment from God was primarily what I needed to focus on. I still researched but didn't get into it too deeply by being more careful about how much and what I read. I then prayed that God would give me wisdom to decide what information to take on board.

It's impossible for us to work everything out. While on this Earth, there will always be unanswered questions and there are many times I've had to learn to live with that. The complexity of our bodies can be a hindrance when we are wanting answers, but God designed us and when we think about how well each intricate little part and detail all work together, it's absolutely amazing. Instead of being frustrated with the complexity of my body I decided I should praise and thank God for it as the psalmist did.

'Thank you for making me so wonderfully complex! Your workmanship is marvelous—how well I know it'. (Psalm 139:14 NLT).

'I praise you because I am fearfully and wonderfully made; your works are wonderful; I know that full well.' (Psalm 139:14).

In my desperate search to get well, I put things into practice that I read or that other Christians felt was what I should do to get well. At times when I felt very ill, I tried anything that even gave me a glimmer of hope of feeling just even a little better. I spoke out healing scriptures, which I recited for one month as a result of someone telling me I would be well if I did this. I thought, I had nothing to lose, it was worth a try. But one month later I felt no different. I spoke to different parts of my body, for example, "Bowels be well, be healed in Jesus's name." I imagined my sickness on Jesus, imagined I'm well, praised God, thanked him, prayed against the spirit of infirmity. You name it, I tried it. I didn't want to miss any chance of being healed.

I don't believe these things are wrong and I still practice some of them now. However, if nothing else, they helped me to have a positive mindset and have given me hope. It's not just about reciting the Word and it being head knowledge but allowing it to be absorbed in your spirit. Scripture declaration also builds faith. '*Faith comes by hearing, and hearing by the word of God*' *(Romans 10:17 KJV)*. Hearing the Word audibly enables God's Word to penetrate our spirit, causing faith to rise. It's about letting our faith in His Word become more of a reality to us than we can see in the natural.

Sometimes there are no right and wrong answers. My journey has been about trying different methods, so to speak. It's partly like everything in life, what is right for one person isn't for another, and what works for one person docsn't necessarily work for another. After a lot of years of searching and applying, etc., I finally came to the realisation that listening to the Holy Spirit is a big help and often He will show us what is right for us personally, as individuals. I realised it's about not necessarily striving to be well, but giving it to God and allowing His healing to manifest in His way and His timing. Receiving healing is something I'm still working on. I learnt to rely on God's authority to show me the way forward by revealing to me what I can do to help myself. It's about getting the right balance by allowing God to do His part and us doing ours.

During my time with chemical sensitivity, I became desperate at times. I longed to be well, free from pain, frustration and fatigue; free from every day being a constant struggle and a battle. I kept plodding on at work through days and days of feeling sick and just wanting to give up. I could have easily given in and just stayed at home. If it wasn't for the example my parents demonstrated to me when I was growing up, this might have been the case. They believed in earning their money by working hard. I am pleased they had given me my determination to push through, press on and 'carry on regardless,' which sounds like a title of one of those "Carry On" films. Being brought up to be a fighter along with my strong sense of motivation, helped immensely. But I was exhausted. When it reached a point where I was ill every week, I didn't know how much longer I'd be able to carry on.

For many years I've tried to function like a well person partly because I didn't have a medical diagnosis. I didn't allow my ill health to stop me serving in church as I had a desire to serve God and it helped me feel more part of the church family. However, I now realise I have to accept my limitations and I don't feel guilty for what I'm unable to accomplish. God understands our limitations and doesn't expect more from us than we are capable of giving. He has a job and purpose for every one of us no matter what our circumstances are.

Part 2

My Wellbeing Journey

Confidence in Christ

Towards the beginning of 2014, I went through what seemed at that point, to be the most difficult experience of my life. Despite working with the same staff for years without any problems, suddenly things started taking a turn for the worst because of a staffing structure change within management. I was experiencing bullying and it didn't take long for it to become clear I was no longer wanted in the job. It appeared that my face didn't fit any more. I don't feel it's right to go into all the details here, but I sought advice from a solicitor who confirmed I was experiencing 'religious persecution'; persecution for being a Christian.

'In fact, everyone who wants to live a godly life in Christ Jesus will be persecuted'. (2 Timothy 3:12). *'Blessed are you when people insult you, persecute you and falsely say all kinds of evil against you because of me. Rejoice and be glad, because great is your reward in heaven' (Matthew 5:11).* The enemy (Satan) was at work. Work politics came into it as well but, as Christians we are blessed and favoured, that's why we are targeted. I understood that people can become our enemies by persecuting us because they witness the favour of God on our lives. Others can be resentful because of what God has done for us. By being who Christ changed us to be, for example, practicing honesty, this can convict others of their wrong doing. Also, if people don't like your faith, they may hate you for it. Therefore, they may go to extremes to get you into trouble or

embarrass you. God's Word always has something to comfort us. *"Do not be afraid of them [or their hostile faces], For I am with you [always] to protect you and deliver you," says the LORD.' (Jeremiah 1:8, AMP).*

During this time, I stayed close to Jesus and spoke the relevant scriptures out every morning to remind me of Gods promises and get them in my spirit to strengthen me. When you're close to God, you don't feel like problems can destroy you. *'We are hard pressed on every side, but not crushed; perplexed, but not in despair; persecuted, but not abandoned; struck down, but not destroyed.' (2 Corinthians 4:8).* As soon as I woke up in the morning, I changed some of the scriptures I declared out loud into a personal declaration. The following are some of those I used, taken from the NIV Bible:

'I will be strong and courageous. I am not be afraid or terrified because of them, for the Lord my God goes with me; he will never leave me nor forsake you.' (Deuteronomy 31:6).

"If God is for me, no one can be against me,' (Romans 8:31).

'Because you are sending me out as a sheep amongst wolves, I am as wise as a serpent and as innocent as a dove' (Matthew 10:16).

'I am strong through the grace that God gives me in Christ Jesus,' (2Timothy 2:1).

'Nothing in all creation can separate me from Gods love for me in Christ Jesus our Lord!'(Romans 8:39).

'You will strengthen me, help me and surely uphold me with your righteous right hand.' (Isaiah 41:10).

'I am not letting evil conquer me but I am conquering evil with good.' (Romans 13:21).

'I'm doing all I can to live in peace with everyone,' (Romans 13:8).

'I am strong in the Lord and in his mighty power.' (Ephesians 6:10).

I also regularly spoke out Psalm 91 for protection.

I could quite easily have taken on the victim mentality, because at times I certainly felt like one. But I needed to keep reminding myself that the Holy Spirit was training me up and changing me to be more like Jesus and be more than a conqueror. When I looked inwards at myself, I had feelings of inadequacy, inferiority and insecurity. But looking to Jesus made me feel strong enough to get through the situation. It can be so easy to feel sorry for yourself, seeing yourself as 'Poor Me.'
God kept lifting me up, only to be knocked down again, causing me to experience more stress.

It appeared that certain members of staff were doing all they could in their power to grind me down and make me resign. Because I was regularly getting pulled up for things I'd always done, which had become, all of a sudden unacceptable, I was going to work in fear of what would be thrown at me next. Fear can cause us to lose perspective, blowing things out of proportion by making things seem bigger than what they really are. It can be a bit like looking through a magnifying glass. We can't control what others think of us so I know it's easier said than done but the best thing to do is to let it go. As the saying goes, 'let go and let God', Don't concern yourself with it. In Luke 10:16, Jesus told his disciples that the one who rejects them rejects Him. And Christians are His disciples.

Jesus endured the pain of being falsely accused and didn't feel the need to defend himself. He gave me the right words to say when I needed them. I was aware that God knew the truth and he would have my back. I prayed in the office when alone, speaking in tongues, while anointing the place with oil. I put oil on the walls and under the desks and chairs.

We wouldn't be human if we didn't have some periods in our lives when we weren't stressed, feeling anxious or down, as it's part of life. It becomes a problem when anxiety occurs every day, as it was for me. If stress becomes chronic, it effects our immune system and energy levels. Eventually I had to give in and go on the sick for just over two months, due to anxiety and severe stress.

One lady at Church got a word from God for me, *'Don't battle the work situation, don't fight it, just use this time on the sick to rest in His presence'*. She saw a picture of me with my mouth open laughing. It again reminded me, *'The battle is the Lord's.'* Now I know that my laughing was the victory that God gave me over the situation when He provided my miracle breakthrough and delivered me from that work place. Was I laughing! Time was needed away from the situation for me to heal and be strengthened in body, mind and spirit. In Isaiah 41:10, God promises to help and strengthen us.

In January 2014 when I attended 'Band of Sisters' at Church which concentrated on praying for each person in the group, one at a time and giving them any words or pictures, that God showed us. I was blessed by how God spoke to me. I was given Psalm 91 again, which became a psalm I often prayed on a morning for protection. It was given at a time when I was suffering immense stress due to several life events happening, one after another.

I was also given, *'The joy of the Lord is my strength' (Neh. 8:10).* Another lady prayed for me that through this stress (due to bullying at work) I will look to what the Lord is doing and is going to do. My prayer has been "Lord make me into what you want me to be." I felt God was saying "I'm making you into a prayer warrior. I'm teaching you how to praise me, depend on me, lean on me with your whole being. Look to Me for all your answers. I will guide you and show you the way. I will strengthen you and uphold you". God said, "Ask me for what you want. I want not just a friendship but a marriage". God was drawing me into a deeper and closer relationship with Him. I felt I needed to focus fully on God and remember that we are in a spiritual battle but the battle is the Lord's. God's perfect peace that surpasses all understanding was prayed over me. It's great to have prayer support from other Christians. It really helps to lift us and enable us to carry on.

Eventually after some time on the sick, God gave me enough strength to return to work. This was a difficult decision to make as I wasn't sure how the staff were going to be with me. Even though the persecution and bullying had stopped, it didn't prove to be easy and the whole experience was a daily struggle. But God gave me what I needed to get me through it and remain at work.

I carried on being nice towards those who hadn't been nice to me, only speaking to me when they had to. Even though it wasn't easy, I obeyed what God commanded us to do, as stated in the Bible. *'But I tell you, love your enemies and pray for those who persecute you'. (Matthew 5:43,44). 'Bless those who persecute you; bless and do not curse.' (Romans 12:14). Do not repay evil with evil or insult with insult. On the contrary, repay evil with blessing, because to this you were called so that you may inherit a blessing. (1 Peter 3:9).* The reason for this is that we will be heaping coals of fire on their heads. Another explanation is that they will feel ashamed of themselves for how they have treated you. These were the scriptures that taught me how to treat those that had become my enemies. I prayed blessings over them, prayed for their salvation and chose to be nice to them.

Loving them was the hardest part. How do you love people who you've come to dislike? I could only do it with God's help. I read somewhere that love is an action, not always a feeling. We don't tend to have much control over our feelings but loving someone can mean not talking bad of them, not wishing them any harm and hoping the best for them. It can also mean doing something for them. He helped me to show kindness by not reacting in an ungodly way. *'We love because he first loved us' (1 John 4:19).* Without God I would have reacted differently according to the human flesh with anger and hatred for my colleagues who'd treat me unkindly and unfavourably.

It was in knowing there was a lesson behind the pain that gave me the endurance to carry on. God often puts us in situations in order to test us by seeing how we will respond. *'Consider it pure joy, my brothers, when you encounter trials of many kinds, because you know that the testing of your faith produces perseverance.' (James 1:3).* Tough times teach us perseverance.

The Holy Spirit spoke to me during this difficulty in February 2014 with a message to stop trying to work things out. *'Not by might nor by power, but by my Spirit, says the LORD Almighty.' (Zechariah 4:6).* As I mentioned earlier, He will fight for us. I needed to trust in Him and believe that the Lord had better things for me. It wasn't might or power that could change the situation, it was only His spirit that could do that. His spirit works when we pray.

In one way, going through this situation was a blessing, as it taught me so much. I often think about persecuted Christians in other countries who are beaten, tortured and imprisoned for their faith. What I went through is nothing compared to that, but it was a massive ordeal that made me ill. I can't comprehend how anyone can live through worse and survive. Its only by the grace of God. They are desperately in need of our prayers.

Trusting in God through the process became a big part of my journey. A confidence was developed in me to stand as it says in Ephesians 10:6 and not be defeated and to persevere and trust in God, when all I felt like doing was quitting. When I didn't think I could carry on anymore God gave me the strength that I needed. *'My grace is sufficient for you, for my power is made perfect in weakness.' (2 Corinthians 12:9).* He encouraged me when I felt discouraged. Children go through their life with little fear of falling or injuring themselves. Faith in God is about having that child-like acceptance that everything will work out for the best. God said, *'Truly I tell you, unless you change and become like little children, you will never enter the kingdom of heaven.' (Matthew 18:3).* Children don't doubt but put their full trust in and believe whatever they are told. It was very difficult for me, as doubt always crept in.

I believe that if God wants us to move on, He will close and open doors accordingly. I had always loved my job until these difficulties arose. However, by God allowing this to happen, I knew it could be God's way of moving me out of that work place.

I prayed a lot, tested the waters and attempted to look for another job. Meanwhile, I remained trusting in God's promise that says; *'With man this is impossible, but with God all things are possible.' (Matthew 19:26).* I then said, "God, surely you don't want me to be unhappy like this, so please sort it out." I put my hope in God, knowing He was in control and left him to sort it out. *Psalm 62:5-8* sums this up.

'Let all that I am wait quietly before God, for my hope is in him.
He alone is my rock and my salvation, my fortress where I will not be shaken.
My victory and honor come from God alone.
He is my refuge, a rock where no enemy can reach me.
O my people, trust in him at all times.
Pour out your heart to him,

for God is our refuge.'

When we are resting in God's strength nothing can shake us.

I prayed for what seemed a very long time and waited for a solution. Eventually in December 2014, when the Darlington contract was up for tender, we were told it had been won by another company. Tendering is a formal process where businesses are invited to bid for contracts from public or private sector organisations. Straight away I knew that God was in it. My colleagues' actions had backfired on them. As it says in Galatians *'Do not be deceived: God cannot be mocked. A man reaps what he sows'(Galatians 6:7).* They attempted to cause me to leave the job but as it happened it was them that lost the very job that they loved. We waited to find out if we had a job. In the meantime, the other 3 staff decided to remain working for the same company in other areas. As it happened, I was the only who transferred to the new organization (the office happened to be literally around the corner from my previous one). God opened a door when I was unable to see any way out. My prayer was answered, God had worked my miracle. He made a way where there appeared to be no way, as he did for the Israelites when he parted the sea for them to cross and reach safety, away from their enemies who were chasing them. It was like a dream come true.

The new company and the staff were more than I ever thought possible. Everyone used to say that they'd never worked anywhere else where staff were so nice and all got on so well together. God had given me double blessings for my troubles, because I'd remained faithful to Him. It can be all too easy, in these kinds of situations, to allow our fleshly nature to take over, which can cause us to sin or make the wrong decisions. David describes it perfectly, what God did for me, in 2 Samuel 17-25:

'He reached down from on high and took hold of me;
   he drew me out of deep waters.

He rescued me from my powerful enemy,
   from my foes, who were too strong for me.

They confronted me in the day of my disaster,
   but the Lord was my support.

He brought me out into a spacious place;
   he rescued me because he delighted in me.

The Lord has dealt with me according to my righteousness;
   according to the cleanness of my hands he has rewarded me.

For I have kept the ways of the Lord;
   I am not guilty of turning from my God.

All his laws are before me;

I have not turned away from his decrees.

*I have been blameless before him
and have kept myself from sin.*

*The Lord has rewarded me according to my
righteousness,
according to my cleanness in his sight.'*

When an unrelated situation arose that caused me
stress and anxiety, I was much more prepared to
deal with it. As a result of our neighbours' ongoing
constant actions regarding their dog, my husband
and I became very stressed. It then became a choice
of whether to accept it or approach them and
discuss it. We decided to explain to them kindly
how over time we'd became increasingly stressed.
The woman's reaction was one of defense and
hostility and her attitude was very unpleasant,
which took us totally by surprise. The couple were
not apologetic and didn't seem at all interested in
trying to sort out the problem.

I felt offended and, as a result of her attitude, I
started getting periods of bad anxiety. The anxiety
came from the fear of a worse reaction from these
people or what they may do to us. *'Fear of man will
prove to be a snare, but whoever trusts in the lord is
kept safe.' (Proverbs 29:25).* The best way to break
the spirit of fear is by coming against it with
boldness. Situations like this can be a test from God
to see if we are going to handle it His way. I then

made a choice to do what it says in the Bible to forgive and pray for them, praying that God would bless them. As I did this, my negative feelings for this couple then changed. I remembered what God said in His Word and in Psalm 91 so I spoke this out along with certain scriptures I'd learnt from my previous experience. I was so much more prepared and focused on God's care and protection for me, that the anxiety completely left almost straight away. Even though I was having to see these people I didn't have to work with them.

Eventually I was then able to speak to this couple and be pleasant to them, while overlooking their faults. I was able to focus on the fact that God loves me and has a plan and purpose to bring me out of situations like this, stronger and better. I got my joy and peace back that the enemy tried to steal from me. I knew that the reason God had allowed it to happen was to change me as a person, as I also learnt not to take offence, not to overthink things or dwell on the negative, but to pray and trust God that he would provide a solution to this problem. It's about laying aside our ideas of how to sort a difficult situation and allowing God to act. By allowing someone's actions or words to upset us, we enable them to control us. If we don't deal with offence, it can tie us down to unforgiveness. I had to let it all go.

God took me by complete surprise again, considering the couple had been married for many years and all of a sudden, he and the dogs were nowhere to be seen. We later learnt he'd moved out. I questioned whether God would answer prayers in this kind of way. I will clarify we didn't pray any harm, we only prayed for God to provide a solution or for the dog to quieten down.

At the beginning of December 2019 after being on sick leave with mental health (due to my breakdown) for just over ten months I was called into work for a meeting. Being aware I could lose my job had a detrimental effect on my mental health. Even though I asked if they could wait until January 2020 to make a decision as I'd just started some new medication, I was told then that I would be dismissed. It's heart breaking when circumstances prevent you from doing the job you love. In addition, the thought of claiming benefits filled me with dread when I'd worked all my life and especially when my job involved support others through this process. Although, I'm also aware that God closes doors for a reason, I still struggled to come to terms with it at first. However, it was then that I witnessed God using me which was confirmation I was where He wanted me.
Over time it became apparent that losing my job was the best thing that could have happened to me. I changed my job on Facebook to 'I'm a disciple of Jesus at I work for God'. You are never redundant when you work for God. That's my calling in life; to be God's disciple and to be used for His glory.

I could now relate much better to others who were experiencing mental health problems. I found myself being an encourager and support to others not only in person but also in Facebook support groups. When the Holy Spirit prompts me by putting someone on my heart or something in my mind, I take the opportunity. During a conversation with a Facebook friend, I stated that some people just post about themselves but I like to try and post things that I feel will encourage others. She said, 'That's why we get a 'jewel moment' (my nick name) each time. You are well named and God uses His jewels in many delightful ways". I thought that was lovely.

Highly Sensitive

A highly sensitive person (HSP) is someone who is thought to have an increased central nervous system sensitivity to emotional, physical, or social stimuli. HSP is a personality trait coined by Dr. Elaine Aron, a psychotherapist. There are thought to be only approximately 15 to 20 percent HSPs in the world of which 30 per cent are extroverts.

It can make life very difficult being a HSP. Traits include being easily overwhelmed, a low threshold of stimulation, love of quiet environments and nature, deep caring attitude, strong intuition, dislike of large groups and crowds, need of rest and alone time, sensitivity to sound, smell, and light, dislike of conflict, trouble fitting in, and have a desire to help others.
Being HSP can be draining somewhat and overwhelming as you feel emotions more intensely

than others. I've always said I have the ability to feel peoples' emotions and to experience what they are experiencing. I have the ability to place myself in another person's shoes and feel the emotions they are feeling. Caring is in my nature. It's a trait I've inherited from my mum. My dad also exhibits those qualities.

However, there is a down side to being HSP in that criticism and offence can hit us harder. I'm moved to tears easily. People haven't been able to understand how I can, as a friend put it 'cry at the drop of a hat' if I hear someone telling me a sad story or a traumatic event that has happened to them or that they are currently experiencing. Most people haven't understood this but it's how God made me. It's a trait I've inherited from my dad. A friend couldn't understand why I am so emotional. I kept telling her it was just the way I am, it's in my genes, it's how God made me. She still struggled to understand it having the view that it wasn't normal. However, it is normal for me. After thirteen years of friendship, she understands it. Crying is a good thing as it releases pent up emotions.

I've never embraced my crying but tried to fight it and conceal it as I'd always felt somewhat different (abnormal) to others and I wanted to fit in. I've been told I'm too sensitive. I saw it as an embarrassment to cry at things that no one else seemed to find upsetting. Therefore, I tried to hold back the tears and hide them. However, it says in God's Word that he bottles our tears. Also, Jesus wept out of compassion and empathy after Mary and Martha's brother died, even though He knew He was going to raise him from the dead. He can identify with how we are feeling and has compassion for us when we are upset.

I remember crying once after visiting a client in the mental health ward when I was saying goodbye. I then bumped into the manager of the mental health team as I was leaving and told her how embarrassed I felt crying in front of the client. Her reply was, 'well at least she knows you care'. That made me feel a whole lot better. And my caring nature is what gave me that special relationship with those people I supported. One of them wrote me a letter once and in it he wrote 'you didn't treat me as just another number.'

The world can seem overwhelming. Our emotions seem to be on high alert when interacting with people. But that's what gave me the passion to be good at my job as a community support worker.

In one way I'm thankful to God for my sensitive nature as it's what makes me compassionate, loving and caring. Highly sensitive people are needed in the world to be what others can't be. It would be a boring world if we were all alike.

I've been seen to be too soft with people and been told I'm too kind or too nice. I've prayed for a strengthening of my heart and emotions and protection over my mind, especially with the job I did in supporting all kinds of people with all sorts of issues and problems. I prayed against taking offence and often pray I will see people as God sees them. As a result, God has strengthened me, while still protecting my heart from being hardened. The Holy Spirit is our best Teacher and is teaching me all the time. After praying the above, I found myself in some very difficult situations with clients and one situation with an angry mother.

People I supported were sometimes stronger characters, more assertive and forceful than myself. Each situation was aimed at showing me to be incompetent but in each instance, I knew I hadn't done anything wrong. I was reminded that I work with damaged people. I was able to see things from a different perspective, from the other persons perspective and not take it personally.

My husband told me, "You're too kind, you need to speak with confidence". I later felt the Holy Spirit saying, "you've got to learn to defend yourself." It's amazing when Jesus gives us the answers we need. I felt the difficult situations I'd been in at work were an answer to my prayers in order to teach me to stand up for myself.

HSP can be vulnerable to being manipulated by others. We just want to help so can become over involved and not see their motive of trying to take advantage for their own benefit. That has been partly what has caused me to become emotionally involved with men who were addicts. One was alcohol dependent and emotionally abusive and another was a compulsive gambler. Their extra attention towards me because they were insecure about themselves made me feel good about myself, special and loved. But the relationships were volatile. An addiction can turn someone into a horrible person. For example, a person can be very nice when not drinking but become abusive when they have had a few drinks. Dealing with that was stressful in itself. It's like living with a 'Jekyll and Hyde'.

That, as well as the emotional abuse and stress of university, caused me to feel depressed and suffer bad mood swings. At times I was feeling suicidal but I knew there was no way I would act on it. When my boyfriend took me to the doctors the GP told him that it must be difficult for him coping with me. I remember thinking, 'he's played a huge part in me being like that'. I was diagnosed with a mild form of what was manic depression, now known as bipolar. I was on tablets for a couple of months then was okay without them after that. I remember thinking that I didn't know one could feel this good. I think I'd had depression for a very long time before I realised it. It was during this time I became a Christian so that seemed to help with my moods.

You may be interested to learn this is in the book "Readers digest. 1,001 Home remedies" research indicates that, in a group of 4,000 older people, those attending a church service resulted in them being half as likely to be depressed as those who didn't. Another research conducted by Columbia University found that out of those who attend church and value religion 90 per cent were less likely to suffer depression than those who are none religious.

However, I don't regret those experiences I've mentioned as it's what helped me to understand better those with addictions and people in abusive relationships whom I supported. It felt as if I had been in training for my job as a community support worker for most of my life.

I got a word from a good friend called Stuart once. He told me he felt that at my job I'm just in training. That God is preparing me for what He has for me which is so much more. My gifts will be used and I will flourish. I've been in preparation. What an encouragement!

Forgiveness

Emotional healing depends on our willingness to forgive. Forgiveness and mercy have the potential to restore broken relationships and heal broken hearts. It's important for our own peace too.

Most people carry negative feelings such as shame, guilt, blame, bitterness, resentment and pride. We don't need to be held in bondage by resentment when others hurt us, as God can set us free. If we don't forgive, then these feelings weigh us down. Forgiveness doesn't excuse peoples' behaviour but prevents their behaviour from destroying your heart. Forgive others, not because they deserve it, but because you deserve peace.

'See to it that no one falls short of the grace of God and that no bitter root grows up to cause trouble and defile many.' (Hebrews *12:15).* Bitterness can be the result of holding on to grudges. It can be like a small root growing into a great tree. The longer we hold on to it, the more it can consume us. When we feel offended, and mull over what the other person has said or done to us, it can put us into the enemy's hands, as it makes us dwell on the negative. It then feeds into how we are already feeling for example upset, hurt, angry.

We need to let go and give these negative feelings to God before they have chance to grow into anything deeper, spreading and affecting us like a cancer. It was stated in the 'Word for Today' devotional, when asked which emotions contribute most to physical illness, a group of eminent doctors said that it is anger and unforgiveness. That's because over time they release deadly toxins into your body. One doctor said, "It's not what you are eating, but what's eating you that threatens your health." I believe it is what you are eating as well. You will see it when reading how diet has contributed to my improved health and wellbeing.

Charles F. Glassman in an article called The Elimination Diet talks about removing these negative emotions of anger, regret, resentment, guilt, blame and worry. Then watching your life and health improve. The Holy Spirit can remove and heal these hurts. With his help everything is possible.

There are feelings we carry towards ourselves as well as those we carry as a result of what others have done to us. Guilt reminds us we've made a mistake. But we all make them and need to be able to forgive ourselves. We can live with negative feelings eating away at us or choose to forgive like it says in His Word.

We are all sinners and can fail God on a regular basis often without even knowing it. The Bible informs us what acts are sinful but this isn't an exhaustive list. '*The acts of the flesh are obvious: sexual immorality, impurity and debauchery; idolatry and witchcraft; hatred, discord, jealousy, fits of rage, selfish ambition, dissensions, factions and envy; drunkenness, orgies, and the like. I warn you, as I did before, that those who live like this will not inherit the kingdom of God.' (Galatians5:19)*. However, God in His grace forgives us if we confess what we have done wrong then ask His forgiveness. *'If we confess our sins, He is faithful and just and will forgive us our sins and purify us from all unrighteousness.' (1 John 1:9)*.

During my breakdown I was suffering from a great deal of guilt and condemnation which is apparently quite common with depression. Guilt because I was having to rely on my husband and parents to help me get through the day. I couldn't accept the extent of the lack of independence it caused. Guilt that I was causing them so much upset seeing me so unwell. Guilt that I wasn't getting better as fast as they would have liked. It takes time to get over a mental breakdown. However, we can bring all that guilt, shame and emotional pain to Jesus (the one who died to take those feelings away), give it to Him, ask for His forgiveness and that He will replace it with His peace.

I was also dealing with the rejection of losing a friend I'd had for years who told me she no longer had time to meet with me. I've heard it's a common occurrence to lose friends when you suddenly aren't able to do what you used to. But to my surprise in God's goodness, He has provided me with several other wonderful friends to replace that one.

God doesn't treat us according to our worthiness. He wants to lavish His unconditional love on us. The mercy and grace He shows us enables us to have second chances. Jesus has his arms wide open waiting for us to come to Him and repent.

God looks at our heart and not our short comings. Knowledge of this enabled me to not only know but eventually feel I am good enough and that with God, mistakes don't result in condemnation.

'Therefore, there is now no condemnation for those who are in Christ Jesus,' (Romans 8:1). It was so comforting to have the reassurance of knowing that when I'd done something wrong, I was still accepted by God.

Forgiveness isn't an act of our emotions, but of our will. It's about handing the situation over to God to deal with. When we choose to forgive, a heavy weight can be lifted to make us feel lighter. During my healing journey there have been many people I've chosen to forgive. These are members of the medical profession who I felt had neglected me. Others include colleagues, a Chinese doctor, people and friends for saying things that were well-meaning but hurtful. In my line of work, I'd learnt to deal with all sorts of people including those with psychopathic traits, narcissists, emotional Vampires (those who suck the life out of you if you let them). An emotional vampire is someone who makes you question your beliefs and perception of reality, manipulates, or uses other emotionally controlling tactics to diminish another person. I've come across verbal abuse from clients and others. I've had people hurl abusive anger towards me all because they didn't get their own way. I liken it to a "child spitting their dummy out". It can be upsetting at the time but I'm aware that these people have issues and I know not to take it personally as they will be doing the same to the next person. It can sometimes be the enemy working through them as a way of trying to upset us by hurting us and putting us down. I once read a quote stating, 'You can trust the person but you can't trust the devil inside' which I think can sometimes sum it up. Hurting people hurt people. These people are hurting so out of their brokenness they hurt you in return. We need to keep short accounts with God, continue to be easy on people and forgive. It is a choice we can all make. Forgiveness doesn't mean excusing their behaviour.

What I would say is that we don't have to take abuse but we can forgive whilst keeping a certain distance from that person if it's possible to do so. Why should we allow ourselves to be anyone's emotional punch bag? We can also choose to walk away, or put the phone down, then deal with them when they have calmed down. It is our choice whether we want to remain in a relationship with a person who is abusive. But we need to take care of ourselves and remember that tolerating abuse can be detrimental to our own mental health.

However, we also need wisdom as we may need to rethink our relationship with the person who harmed or hurt us. God doesn't want division but He doesn't want us to put ourselves in a place where we can continuously be hurt either. The other person may not acknowledge they are in the wrong or may fail to even see they are in the wrong. I've made choices where I've chose to still speak to the person but chose not to be in a friendship with them anymore. This is because I've been aware their behaviour wasn't going to change and I've needed to protect my mental health.

We need to learn not to take offense which I'm aware can be extremely difficult. I don't win every time, but God helps me to do that better. God has helped me not to be offended or upset in many circumstances where I would humanly feel that way without His intervention. In Luke 6:29 God tells us to turn the other cheek meaning that God will handle things. I have learnt to develop a 'thicker skin' but keep a soft heart.

Words spoken against us can be some of the most hurtful, but if we trust in God these don't have to cause any lasting damage. People may hurt us unintentionally and even though we are feeling hurt they may not even know they have hurt us. *'Make allowance for each other's faults, and forgive anyone who offends you. Remember, the Lord forgave you, so you must forgive others.' (Colossians 3:13).* Often people can be having a bad day, suffering mental health problems or anything can be going on without us knowing, e.g., a cashier in the shop may be short with you for what appears to be no reason but could have just found out her brother has been diagnosed with cancer. It's so easy to judge people. However, God, for a good reason, commands us to not to judge. God has been gracious to us through everything we have done wrong. Everyone makes mistakes and people often have issues as they are affected by their past. *'Do not judge, or you will be judged. For with the same judgment you pronounce, you will be judged; and with the measure you use, it will be measured to you.'(Matthew 7:1-2).* We have to remember that we have also got our shortcomings. *'Why do you look at the speck in your brother's eye, but fail to notice the beam in your own eye?' (Luke 6:41).*

God commands us to forgive and there are consequences if we don't. He then won't forgive us. *'But if you do not forgive others their sins, your Father will not forgive your sin.' (Matthew 6:15).* When people have hurt me, I try and focus on these scriptures, remembering that none of us are perfect. But Jesus still loved everyone when He was on this earth and still does now.

Forgiveness is often a process and doesn't happen all at once. We may need to keep on forgiving time and time again, as thoughts enter our heads. I've found that speaking out forgiveness when I don't feel like it can lead to a change of feelings. Feelings follow actions. If the experience is very painful, often prayer or Christian counselling is required to help people through this process. But if we ask God, He gives us the grace and strength to forgive.

I've heard of people forgiving others, and then, as a result of that, receiving physical healing for themselves. One Pastor gave an example of this in his sermon. He had a tooth problem which the dentist couldn't solve. He forgave himself as well as the dentist for failing to heal the tooth which made it worse! As a result, the pain disappeared. One thing that has often worked for people is writing down what someone said or did to hurt them.

Asking God to help them forgive and heal the pain, and then burning the piece of paper.

Emotional Wellbeing

According to Psychology Today, the definition of emotional well-being is "the ability to practice stress management techniques, be resilient, and generate the emotions that lead to good feelings." Hobbies can be therapeutic and bring a sense of wellbeing.

Having the allotment had been somewhat of a challenge in the experience of growing as well as having the time and energy that it requires. It became a burden at times, having to go when we didn't feel up to it, to water etc. I remember forcing myself to go and then wanting to come home half an hour later as my body was aching so badly and I was needing to sit down and rest. For these reasons we've had a discussion on many occasions about whether to give it up. However, a few years later we were so pleased to still have it. My husband was so good as he let me do just as much as I could manage and then bought some chairs so I could then sit and rest while he worked. I enjoyed the learning aspect of it by reading the books. I was part of an allotment group on Facebook and it has done me the world of good. It's so interesting looking at photos of others allotments and it's a place where people can post photos of vegetables that aren't doing well and others tell you what the problems could be. It was lovely to have a hobby that we as a couple could share together and it had proved to be so therapeutic. One of my jobs was the weeding and it's surprising how therapeutic that can be in itself.

After my breakdown we made the decision to give up the allotment as my husband couldn't manage it alone and ever since my healing I struggled with unpredictable severe fatigue. We have no doubt it was the right decision and we don't regret it. It was a huge commitment and my husband said it means he can use the time for our garden which was being neglected.

I learnt to find value and beauty in small things. This helped to make me feel better; for example; sitting in the front room when the sun is coming in, looking out of my bedroom window at trees when ill in bed or gazing at the flowers is so relaxing. My husband very rarely buys me bunches of flowers but plants them in pots in the garden for me, which I love.

We had a barrel in the garden that collected water and it was wonderful watching the birds having a bath in it. We now have a lovely bird bath, which my parents bought us. All these things are therapeutic and contribute to healing, by giving us a sense of wellbeing. It's surprising how little things like this can lift your mood and brighten your day. I started looking for a bird table but then my husband said he'd make me one, which took some time as he was busy with other things. When I finally did get my bird table it felt like a luxury. However, unfortunately, about two years later I saw a large animal peeping from behind the plant pot twitching its nose. When I mentioned it to my husband, he said he wondered if it was a guinea pig that had escaped from someone's garden. Then a couple of days later we found out what it was when he saw a rat running across our garden, then another one coming over the top of the fence from next door and pinching food from the bird table. It was hilarious to watch but I was very disappointed as this meant we could no longer feed the birds. We put the rat trap on the bird table and tied the scarecrow on that we'd bought for the allotment, to stop the birds going on it.

There are many things to thank God for, not only birds but hot running water, answered prayers, laughter, anything that is good. *"Many, LORD my God, are the wonders you have done, the things you planned for us. None can compare with you; were I to speak and tell of your deeds, they would be too many to declare." (Psalm 40:5).* It is a command of Jesus to praise and thank Him. This causes the enemy to take a step back and flee. *"By him therefore let us offer the sacrifice of praise to God continually, that is, the fruit of our lips giving thanks to his name," (Hebrews 13:15, King James Bible).* And God is worth praising and thanking as He is awesome. He has sustained me, strengthened me, kept me going and comforted me. And all these are His healing. Thanking God and being grateful for who He is and for our blessings, produces in us a positive mindset and can lift our mood. I used to suggest to the clients I worked with to write down at least one thing each day that they are grateful for, to help lift their mood.

One particular day when I'd been struggling very badly with medication withdrawal symptoms a prophecy and prayer invitation for zoom popped up on Facebook that I felt God wanted me to attend. As I was entering, my husband told me, "You are like" I finished his sentence with "a dying swan". On zoom the Christians listened to God and then a lady asked if I had neck pain which I told her I did so they prayed for that. Then others told me what they got which was very encouraging. One man said that I've got the oil of joy and said joy is a weapon that puts you above your enemies. *"The joy of the Lord is your strength"* (*Nehemiah 8:10*). They then asked what I wanted prayer for so I explained my health issues due to mirtazapine withdrawal. Afterwards the lady who prayed informed me that she was helping her dad come off mirtazapine and she was aware how difficult it is. It's just fabulous how God knows what we need and put me in touch with someone who can understand how difficult it is.

Joy is a decision, not a reaction to circumstances. It's about focusing on God's goodness every day. His goodness has been evident in my life in many ways. As joy produces strength, it explains why joy is one of the devil's targets. When you lose your joy, you lose your strength, and then the enemy wins. Our peace and joy are worth fighting for because they are rightfully ours in Jesus. *Peace I leave with you; my peace I give you. I do not give to you as the world gives. Do not let your hearts be troubled and do not be afraid." (John 14:27).* It's a conscious decision to keep check of our hearts and focus on good and positive things. We need to take care of our spiritual health. Once, in 2016, when I was praying about my ill health, God gave me the scripture *'Finally, be strong in the Lord and in his mighty power.' (Ephesians 6:10).*

To overcome attacks from the enemy we must be dependent on God's strength and use our spiritual armour in Ephesians 6. We are vulnerable to being attacked when we are weak, feeling alone, helpless, not connected with other Christians or too focused on our troubles or ill health. When we are going through a difficult time, we must remember to connect with other Christians for support. We should keep our eyes on God and resist the devil as it says in James 4:7, *"Submit yourselves, then, to God. Resist the devil, and he will flee from you."* I often pray against any works of the enemy in my life, our marriage and my body.

Being content in every situation was something I had to learn, just as Paul said he did. *'I have learned to be content whatever the circumstances.' (Phil 4:11).* True contentment doesn't depend on what we have, such as money, belongings, our status or success, but on the feeling inside of us. For me it was about knowing that I was where God had placed me and where he wanted me to be at the time. It's more than a feeling, it's a sense of knowing that God is in control. It's about being in a stressful situation and still having that peace that everything will work out and that '*I can do all things through Christ who strengthens me*' *(Philippians 11:13)* because He will get me through.

During my period of depression, a friend wrote me a poem, which she agreed for me to share. Her poems are inspired by God. Here is a poem that brought great comfort and healing into my life during that period.

I look upon you tenderly
And hear you when you call.
My arms are always open wide
To catch you when you fall.

I walk beside you every day,
I'm there when you're in need.
Don't hesitate to call my name,
For I'm your friend indeed.

I'll never leave you all alone,
I listen to your prayers.
Come, share with me each burden,
Let me wipe away your tears.

I give you strength when you are weak
To help you through each day.
Because I am the Lord your God,

Your friend upon the way.

So, smile, my child, take courage,
Be bold and strong with me.
I died upon the cross for you,
Your Lord of Calvary.

Inspired Christian Poetry by Penny Martin

Self Care

The following are some of the things that have
helped me with my wellbeing and have reduced my
stress over the years:

>Getting enough sleep by listening to my body at
that time. Sometimes I needed more than other
times. Lack of sleep can impact on our health,
immune system and stress levels, leaving us
vulnerable and open to enemy attack.

>Scheduling time to do something we love makes
us feel good and helps us de-stress. It's therapeutic
and takes our minds off negative thoughts and
feelings. I've found having a day out or
attending the cinema with my husband to be very
therapeutic, as it takes the mundane out of everyday
life and routine. Also, just getting out into a
different environment helps our wellbeing and can
lift a low mood.

>Having relaxing hobbies is a help as well, such as crafts, reading, gardening, colouring or jigsaws. Hobbies are a distraction to take our minds off our symptoms, or any problems or worries.

> I find connecting with female friends helpful as they think differently to men. Christian friends can be particularly helpful, as they think along the same lines spiritually and can offer prayer support.

> Exercising brings a relaxed feeling and a sense of wellbeing. It's good for our mental health as well as our physical health, as it produces serotonin which is the feel-good chemical that improves mood. I love walking in nature. Doing this with a friend helped me during lockdown. Pilates has helped my posture and back problems. After years of attending Physio on and off finally receiving the right exercises has reduced the episodes of shoulder and neck pain.

> Deep breathing helps bring relaxation when stressed. 4-6 deep belly breaths slow your heart rate and help you calm down. Some meditation practices include breathing or focusing on your breathe.

> Doing something nice for someone else to support them or brighten their day has helped me to feel that I achieved something worthwhile. I read that it can release the chemical oxytocin, which makes us feel good. Hugging someone for at least 6 seconds can

have the same effect. Many people just need someone to talk to.

> Learning by attending training courses, doing research or learning a new hobby or skill. It keeps life interesting and our brains occupied and active.

> Having a purpose to my day after I'd stopped working helped massively. Most days I make a point of having something on, even if it's only for one or two hours, so it gives me something to look forward to and a structure to my day and week.

> Being assertive has been a massive struggle as I was brought up to be submissive, so I had to learn these skills as well as having the confidence to put them into practice. Not always feeling obliged to say 'yes' and learning to say 'no' has been easier after things started impacting my health. I had to learn to accept that I don't always have the energy levels to always do what people ask and it is critical for my health that I don't exhaust myself. I dislike letting people down, but I've had to let go of guilty feelings when I've said "no" and give them to God.

> Crying has a positive effect. My husband never cries and he thought it was harmful to me. However, it prevents the stress going into our bodies. Even though it isn't a conscious decision to cry, it helps release negative emotions, and makes us feel better. God made tear ducts and tears can be healing, as they have been for me on many an occasion. I hope this encourages those, who might

feel, as I did for a long time, that crying is a negative thing to experience which my husband used to think until he finally accepted my explanation of why it's a good thing.

> Laughter is like medicine. It can reduce stress and provides healing to our bodies. *"A cheerful heart is good medicine, but a crushed spirit dries up the bones,"* (*Proverbs 17:22*). My husband is bit of a character, he is a great laugh without even meaning to be. God certainly knew what I needed when he brought us together. Laughter is known to strengthen the immune system, boost mood, reduce pain and protect us from the damaging effects of stress.

> Detoxing from things that harm our bodies. As well as reducing the obvious chemicals around us such as toiletries and cleaning products I changed all my plastic containers to glass, stopped using cling film etc and started eating organic whenever we could.

It's important to take care of our spiritual health which is a conscious decision and a discipline. Prayer needs to be carried out when things are going well just as much as when they aren't. Like many Christians I've often struggled to keep up regular Bible study. I've realised that if we are struggling in this area, the solution can lie in being creative as it makes our time with God more interesting. This then motivates us to want to spend time with God. If we struggle to get into the Bible for various reasons there are options. Here are some of the things that have helped me:

- Reading a different version of the Bible can bring fresh revelation.
- Listen to the Bible on You Tube or a Bible app.
- Listen to Bible teaching on an area that you are struggling with.
- Read a daily devotional.
- Bible study books that are free from Our Daily Bread (odb.org) and have a space to write with two questions to think about.
- You Version app is free to download and has numerous versions, as well as endless short manageable Bible plans to choose from, videos, verse of the day and a short story to go with that verse. It's also audible.

Meditation

Meditation is something I've never wanted to over complicate, but have felt it beneficial for relaxation, especially during times of stress. I read that ten minutes meditation can keep you relaxed. I have previously used tapes with relaxing music or words but now use You Tube. There is a vast selection of meditations on You Tube ranging from Christian to chronic pain, fibromyalgia, sleep, scriptures, relaxing nature scenes and many others.

I got into the habit of doing short ten minute meditations either focusing on my breath or Jesus. There are some Christian mindfulness videos on You Tube. I sometimes put relaxing music on whilst using the computer. I've become familiar with Mindfulness (a form of meditation) since going on the taster session at Mind and later an eight week course run by the NHS.

According to positivepsychology.com there are five main benefits of mindfulness based on research.

1. Decreases stress.
2. Increases our ability to deal with ill health, making symptoms more manageable.
   Decreases symptoms of
3. depression
4. Improves health

Mindfulness is about keeping our full attention and focus on the present moment which can be whatever we are doing such as washing up or eating. Alternatively, our attention can be on our breathing, relaxing music, sensations in our body or an object such as a candle. If we focus on something, we are eating, such as a raisin which was used as an example in the session, we smelt it first and focused on how it smelt. We then did the same with touch and taste. If other thoughts come into our mind, then we would acknowledge it's there but not dwell on it, allowing it to pass as a bus does when one is standing at the bus stop. It helps with negative thoughts so that you aren't dwelling on them and keeps your thoughts centred on the present instead of the past or the future. It might sound easy but it does take practice. Previously I hadn't been aware that meditating on Jesus or scripture is actually a form of mindfulness.

I've found one of the best and simplest forms of meditation to practice is just to sit in the presence of Jesus and allow His love and peace to surround me. This is also a form of prayer, whereby you are open to hearing from God and listening to what He might have to say as He places thoughts into your mind and brings Bible passages to mind or pictures/visions. One way to know whether it is God speaking to us is to ensure it lines up with scripture from the Bible. I've had a deep sense of relaxation with waves flowing through my body on several occasions, while lying in bed, just focusing on Jesus. It has been beneficial in reducing pain and bringing peace of mind. There is nothing more refreshing and healing for the soul, than time in His presence. I don't get many visions from God but have had the odd one.

In 2015 I saw a vision of an empty field with a gate. Then I received these words, "Open that gate, go in and enter His rest. He is the Shepherd and you are His sheep. Spend time with Him there, reach out and touch Him like the woman with the issue of the blood *(whom Jesus healed)*. Let His spirit touch yours, bathe in that love and peace". *Italics* are my words. Then I felt to thank God that I'm accepted, chosen, loved and forgiven by Him. There is no other love more perfect than the love of God, which has produced healing. God's love is unconditional, and we cannot do anything that would make Him love us any more or any less.

Jesus also said to His disciples, *"Come with me by yourselves to a quiet place and get some rest,"* *(Mark 6:31)*. Especially when life is so busy, it's a good practice to make time for Jesus each day by tuning out any distractions and stresses, to come into Jesus' presence and rest in Him. I must admit it's something I don't always make time to do, but I find it very important to help reduce stress, otherwise we can be overburdened or overworked. Jesus said, "*Come to me, all you who are weary and burdened, and I will give you rest*," (*Matthew 11:28)*. When I've been stressed, it has been difficult to think straight, so I've often forgotten to come to Him. It's been about practice and training. I have had to train myself to get into the habit of doing this as the first port of call. Jesus is our resting place, our shelter from the storm.

Jesus understands our pain and suffering like no one else. As well as turning to Him for healing, we can also turn to Him for comfort and counsel. It's good to talk to Jesus, to tell Him how we feel by being totally honest with Him, then allowing Him to soothe our pain. He will replace our sadness with joy, hopelessness with hope, etc. Giving Him our worries, concerns and burdens can really help our emotional wellbeing.

The Bible tells us to *'cast all your anxiety on him because he cares for you.' (1 Peter 5:7)*. People aren't always available to or capable of showing us compassion for example when we need it, but our loving Father (God) is always there for us. *He* wants a relationship with us so, we need to be intimate with Him. We can spend time with God in many ways. He longs to spend time with us, as a Father does with his children.

In June 2016 my lovely friend Margaret got a word from God for me, *'...in quietness and trust is your strength, but you would have none of it.' (Isaiah 30:15)*. If we are still and quiet before God, taking our minds away from men, the world and our negative emotions, it will give us strength. It's about being peacefully confident that He will give us the strength to face our difficulties.

Margaret also got for me, *'Yet the LORD longs to be gracious to you; therefore, he will rise up to show you compassion. For the LORD is a God of justice. Blessed are all who wait for him!' (Isaiah 30:18)*. Therefore, the LORD must wait for you to come to Him to spend time with Him, so He can show you His love and compassion. We then wait for Him to help us and answer our prayers. This

scripture reminded me that God cannot show us His love and compassion without us first coming to

Him. When I've been distressed, it's been all too easy to try and work things out for myself, forgetting to give my negative feelings to God, not allowing him to help me by making me feel better, bringing me an answer or showing me what I can do to change a situation. On the other hand, difficulties can draw us closer to God. It's only when we draw near to God that our minds are refreshed, and our strength is renewed.

Memorising scripture and meditating on it, is another form of meditation I use. This way scripture gets deep into your soul, into your inner most being. We can then change from the inside out. *'The Spirit gives life; the flesh counts for nothing. The words I have spoken to you, they are full of the Spirit and life,' (John 6:63).* God's word is very powerful. *'For the word of God is alive and active. Sharper than any double-edged sword, it penetrates even to dividing soul and spirit, joints and marrow; it judges the thoughts and attitudes of the heart,'* (Hebrews 4:12). By allowing the Word to change us, we become more like Jesus, getting rid of things that hinder us and disturb our peace.

My husband is the opposite from me. He is almost robotic with his feelings and emotions and often tells me that I should learn to control my emotions by training my brain. I've kept telling him that it isn't possible for me to do that. However, I'm recently learning that this can be possible (apart from when those women's hormones rule), if I allow and ask God to help me. *'With man this is impossible, but not with God; all things are possible with God,' (Mark 10:27).* It's not about denying how I feel, but asking for God's help, while putting all the above principles into practice, speaking out scripture and taking action. It's about moving in the opposite spirit, as this breaks the power the enemy has over us. For example, when I was being criticised, or persecuted I learned to answer gently. If someone treated me badly, I learned to bless them. I learned to endure the enemy's attacks and persevere in spite of them. This breaks the power of the enemy, otherwise we are giving him a foothold. If feeling ill, I try praying against it, before giving in and going to bed. If I feel overwhelmed and as if I can't cope, I declare:

'I'm strong in the Lord and his mighty power.' (Ephesians 6:10).

'I can do all things through Christ, who gives me strength.' (Philippians 4:13 NLT).

'In all these things I am more than a conqueror through him who loved us.' (Romans 8:37).

It's about using the tools that God has given us to stand and letting Him fight the battles. We, as humans, want answers now, but if we give things to God, He will work things out in His timing, and His timing is perfect!

According to Andrew Newberg who studies the relationship between spiritual phenomena and the brain, there are many benefits to meditation as well as prayer. They enhance memory, increase our capacity for compassion, reduces age related brain deterioration and helps us live longer as well as reducing stress.

Stress

Several years ago, I'd been very stressed by several stressful life events occurring at the same time. I started to praise God and one day woke up to find I was completely free from my stress. However, because it felt too good to be true, I kept doubting and thinking the stress was going to return. After a few days I knew that God had healed me and I testified to this in church. It's very productive to be spiritual but it's also wise to be sensible and have a balance and boundaries. Stress is one of the factors that impacts on IBS and can have a tendency to increase my pains. Stress puts stress on the digestive system. What you think and feel effects your gut as it has been described by alternative practitioners as the second brain. Highly sensitive people like myself can be prone to IBS due to thinking about things more deeply and having stronger emotional reactions. We pick up what people are feeling and are over aroused by it. At times I feel people's pain so deeply, that I am moved to tears, even for people I do not know. This is why receiving an answer to prayer for the strengthening of my emotions has been paramount to my healing.

Stress also impacts on our immune system, having a negative effect on healing. However, even if total healing cannot be achieved, we can still reach a place of wellbeing if we focus on Jesus and positive relationships. This can result in contentment and a sense of purpose.

Keeping stress under control has been an ongoing battle and a constant learning process for me, as I'm sure it is for many people. It didn't help with having a stressful job. The Bible talks about our bodies being a Temple '*Do you not know that your body is a temple of the Holy Spirit who is in you, whom you have received from God? You are not your own; you were bought at a price. Therefore, honour God with your bodies,' (1 Corinthians 6:19,20).* Therefore, we need to look after our bodies by taking care of them.

Days' Rest

Rest means to cease work or movement in order to relax, sleep, or recover strength. It's beneficial to have a day's rest, as God did when he'd finished creating the world. '*For in six days the LORD made the heavens and the earth, the sea, and all that is in them, but he rested on the seventh day. Therefore, the LORD blessed the Sabbath day and made it holy.' (Exodus 20:11).* I felt God spoke to me about doing this. I know that when God tells us something, it is for our own good, as He always knows best. Therefore, I obeyed and began to have one day's rest, usually on a Sunday. However, I did struggle with it at first, as all the other days then became busier. Of course, unfortunately, on my day of rest I still have to cook and wash up, and I don't always stick to it religiously. It became so tempting to go shopping if we were passing a supermarket on the way home from church, as it was sometimes easier to shop then, than do it after work on a week day. It's also important to recognise when we are becoming too tired and need to take time out to rest during any day, e.g., if we have had a busy day. *'Then, because so many people were coming and going that they did not even have a chance to eat, he said to them, "Come with me by yourselves to a quiet place and get some rest.' (Mark 6:31).*

At the latter end of December 2019, nine months after my discharge from the Psychiatric hospital and one year after my breakdown, I started to come out of that deep dark depression I'd been in for one year and my anxiety lifted. The only explanation I could find for that was that there were people who were praying for me the whole time I was unwell and never gave up. To those people I will be forever grateful. This scripture comes to mind, *'And the God of all grace, who called you to his eternal glory in Christ, after you have suffered a little while, will himself restore you and make you strong, firm and steadfast.' (1 Peter 5:10).*

I sent my family cards thanking them for always believing in me and never giving up. They had faith in me when I didn't. I've found that God often uses peoples' prayers to bless others when they are struggling to pray for themselves.

My fears disappeared and everything that I'd been hopelessly trying to claw back just returned such as my confidence, self-esteem and driving skills. I felt God say to me, 'I put you through the test to give you a testimony and so that you know I can come through for you and deliver you'. I can safely say my faith is back as strong as it every was before and I've been left with a stronger passion and increased confidence to reach the lost. To share the good news of Jesus with those who don't know him as their Lord and Saviour. I want to live wholeheartedly for Jesus as no one knows what is around the corner.

The biggest support in my emotional recovery and healing has been from my family but also from others who have mental health problems themselves. It's surprising how many people have suffered with depression in the past or are currently living with depression. Even mental health professionals disclosed to me about being on antidepressants themselves. Since I started going out again God has connected me with the right people at the right time, and that has resulted in my healing. He did for me what it states in *Psalm 147:3 'He heals the broken-hearted and binds up their wounds (healing their pain and comforting their sorrow)' AMP.* I was even at a Volunteers Fair where I was standing at a stall when something triggered my emotions. I found it difficult to hold back the tears when a lady from the next stall seeing I was upset, sat me down and just chatted to me for five or ten minutes. God is so good. He never fails us.

I posted something on Facebook about tinnitus and a colleague I worked with years ago shared with me that she suffered with it as well. She allowed me to phone her so that she could share her experience in more detail. For her it had developed suddenly and she was suffering mental health problems as well. It helps to know there are others who understand what you are going through. It normalises things in a way. It was strange to think that we both had been mental health support workers for all those years and then developed similar problems ourselves.

I was aware of what groups and support there was available in the community because of my job. For this reason, a woman I became friends with said I was like a walking library. I did whatever I could to help myself in my recovery journey. I very much believe in accessing all the support you can get if it is going to help in some way. I referred myself to Talking Changes where I attended a group; CBT, (Cognitive Behavioural Therapy) session on Depression. CBT focuses on changing your thoughts which in turn change your behaviour. I also attended some Taster Sessions at Mind in depression, anxiety, mindfulness, building resilience and stress management, which I must say were excellent. I was surprised at how many working people attended those. I think that due to the pressures of life and the working environment these days there is an increase in mental health problems amongst working people. The job I did as a support worker was very different years ago. There were much less pressures involved and it was more laid back. It became more about meeting targets and achieving outcomes and ensuring lots of paperwork was completed.

After losing my job I soon realised that I didn't have to worry about not having a fulfilling life without it. I joined groups such as lipreading, Bible Study, Care and Share Social group, Pilates, aqua aerobics and line dancing. I was out and about enjoying life again. I kept telling people it was a good time to lose my job at the age of fifty as it meant I was able to join groups that Age UK run, which is where I found the Line dancing class. I went to the beginners' class for one hour then the instructor said I could stay and watch for as long as I wanted so I enjoyed watching and listening to the music for another two hours every week. It filled in one afternoon. God also brought lots of new people into my life. People at line dancing were friendly and chatty and Pilates the same.

People at line dancing were sharing their ailments with me and when I offered to pray for them it resulted in generating conversations about my faith as a Christian. I met people at groups where opportunities occurred to share my faith in one way or another. Once, when signing up for a course I met a lady who mentioned the lack of support there was for her daughter who had mental health problems. I saw her the next day and I really felt God wanted me to go over to her but I was in a rush to be somewhere. I remember thinking that if I go over to her, I will be late. However, I didn't want to miss an opportunity to share my faith or be disobedient to God. Therefore, I went to speak to her and she discussed further her struggles with her daughter's mental health. I was able to relate to what she was saying since I'd worked in that field and had similar frustrations as well as personal difficulties myself. I then gave her a copy of what had helped me, my testimony explaining how Jesus and God helped me. She was happy just to talk to someone who understood her struggles. We don't have to do a lot to make a difference in someone's life.

When I was well enough to concentrate to read, I read an excellent book called Depression: The Curse of the Strong that was written by a Christian Psychiatrist. It was interesting because someone recommended the book to me and I'd been looking to buy it online when I discovered I had it on my book shelf. I'd bought it from a charity shop because my job involved supporting people who suffered depression but I hadn't got around to reading it. In the book Dr Tim Cantopher explains that if depression is caused by stress, then it nearly always happens to certain types of people. Those people have a strong conscience, strong sense of responsibility, arc vulnerable to criticism, diligent, a moral strength, sensitive and are reliable. I found it interesting because those match my characteristics. The author explains how depression isn't a sign of weakness but of having tried to remain strong for far too long. He explains how a strong person will tend to deal with challenges that cause stress whereas others would give up on those challenges before they feel too stressed. He goes on to say that strong people work at their peak performance until they feel irritable, exhausted or stressed which can lead to depression. He describes depression as a 'blown fuse.' As a strong person I've always pushed through life challenges thinking, 'I can do this, I can handle it'. Looking back maybe I should have gone 'on the sick' much sooner rather than trying to work until functioning became impossible. But hindsight is a great thing which we can learn a lot from.

I had a couple of Christian healing sessions from a couple I know who are trained in healing and deliverance. They went through repentance with me which involves forgiveness and revoking it which is to unsay it and replace it with the alternative. So, I replaced it by speaking out the scripture, '*I shall not die, but live, and declare the works of the LORD.*' *(Psalm 118:17)*. I even managed to forgive the Osteomyologist for performing the manipulation that caused the tinnitus.

What I've learnt through my battle with depression is that just getting through the day can be as much as you can physically and mentally cope with and can take all you've got. If it isn't possible to do anything else just focus on self-care. I couldn't even do that. Make eating and drinking your first priority. We need to give ourselves credit for our achievements no matter how small it may be. It could be just the achievement of getting a shower or getting dressed if that's what you are struggling with. Do what you can and reward your achievements no matter how small they are. Small tasks can be such a big deal when you are suffering depression. Everything can feel like a chore. If there is any advice, I'd give anyone recovering from a breakdown it would be to just be patient, go easy on yourself, rest when you need to and take each day as it comes whilst keeping your focus on Jesus. *'You will keep in perfect peace all who trust in you, all whose thoughts are fixed on you! Trust in the Lord always, for the Lord God is the eternal Rock.'(Isaiah 26:3-4).*

No one will ever know how much strength it takes to get a shower or get dressed unless they have been in the depths of major depression. It's something you can't explain. But the struggle is much worse if you suffer anxiety at the same time. It's important to remember to pray for strength and perseverance as God can give us those things. On the bad days during my recovery, I tried to focus on the thought that 'it's okay not to be okay.' I chose to rest, allow my body to heal and try and focus on the fact that good days would come around again.

One thing I learnt from Talking Changes is that when we are low in mood, we filter out the good stuff. We either just don't see it, or we discount it. We need to get into the habit of deliberately thinking optimistically. I bought a gratitude journal where I wrote down what I was grateful for each day. It just helps focus on the fact that there are positive things there even if we don't always notice them. I declared over my mind regularly that I have a sound mind, I have a strong mind, my mind is blessed and I have the mind of Christ. I pray that my hormones will be in perfect balance.

I focus on *Jeremiah 29:11 'For I know the plans I have for you,' says the LORD. 'They are plans for good and not for disaster, to give you a future and a hope.'* As God reminded me of it during my recovery. I declared, 'God has a purpose and destiny for my life. He loves me and His plans are for good and not for evil. I choose life and life in all its fullness.' (John 10:10). My husband allowed me to be what I needed to be. It was as if God had given him supernatural patience to accept me as I was at each stage of my recovery. He didn't complain. He allowed me to do what I could at my own pace. If I couldn't do it, I learnt that tomorrow is another day and a day when I might feel differently.

I now have a deeper love and a bigger heart for those suffering mental health problems and suicidal thoughts.
Reasons for Sickness can include the following:
1, It's part of the fallen world we live in. We won't be whole until we see heaven.

2, Generational curses Exodus 20:5-6

3, Unforgiveness. Harbouring bad feelings towards others.

4, Not asking God for healing. Sometimes we can be satisfied and grow to be comfortable with our sickness.

5, Not living a healthy lifestyle eg lack of exercise or poor diet.

6, If we partake of communion in an unworthy manner, we can reap judgement on ourselves which can be that of ill health as suggested in 1 Corinthians 11:28-30

Gods Healing

Healing for me has been a journey. God has been working when I haven't even realised it, guiding me in the right direction and showing me the way forward. God has used many ways to make His healing power available to me; diet and general care of my body, medical care and attention, inner healing of emotional or psychological causes, forgiveness and supernatural healing. There is evidence in the Bible of Jesus performing healing in different ways. He even used mud and a river.

'*After saying this, he spit on the ground, made some mud with the saliva, and put it on the man's eyes. "Go," he told him, "wash in the Pool of Siloam." So, the man went and washed, and came home seeing.' (John 9:6-7).*

'Elisha sent a messenger to say to him, *"Go, wash yourself seven times in the Jordan, and your flesh will be restored and you will be cleansed." But Naaman went away angry and said, "I thought that he would surely come out to me and stand and call on the name of the LORD his God, wave his hand over the spot and cure me of my leprosy" (2 Kings 5:10-11). So, he went down and dipped himself in the Jordan seven times, as the man of God had told him, and his flesh was restored and became clean like that of a young boy.' (2 Kings 5:14).* These examples emphasise the fact that God doesn't always do things the way we expect. He can ask us to do things that don't make sense to us. But as I've said, God always has a reason for everything. He may have wanted to get rid of some pride within Naaman, who knows.

I had so often focused on being physically unwell that it took my eyes off what God was doing. Writing this book has helped me see things more clearly. I can now see how God is healing me in mind, body, soul and spirit. I now understand how my negative emotions, feelings and stress levels can impact on my physical health, without me even realising it. At certain times I was just focused on myself and my problems when I should have been looking outwards to other people and upward to God.

Ever since I was a young girl, I was very shy and grew up with little confidence and self-esteem. I often felt anxious when around people, especially when in group situations, feeling like I wanted to crawl into a hole. As I've said it was when I started working in mental health field, I found out it was a social phobia or social anxiety (another word for it) I had. I had a dread of social gatherings and remember faking a hangover to my parents to avoid attending a family barbeque. I either used to make excuses not to attend socials or when I could, used alcohol as a way of coping.

When I was in my 20's, I used to wonder what the point was in living. I kept thinking, 'Why are we here?' I felt I needed purpose in my life. I used to get bitter when people hurt me and found it very difficult to forgive them. I tried to find happiness from relationships with men but they hurt me and let me down. I used to get easily stressed and often felt down.

I became a Christian at University through attending the Christian Union, after seeing it advertised at the Fresher's Fayre. Being a Christian dramatically helped improve my mental health and after a few months I no longer needed the medication.

I used to see my quietness as a negative characteristic until someone said to me "God made you that way." I was then able to start accepting it as part of me, instead of it being something I needed to change and overcome. I've beat myself up during times when I've felt I haven't had enough of the right words to say to people. However, the Bible states, '*A truly wise person uses few words.*' *(Proverbs 17:27)*. It also makes me a good listener and I've realised that often all people want is someone to talk to and listen to their problems.

When I realised my anxiety was people related, I was conscious that I was nervous about how others viewed me. However, I was never afraid of people I knew loved me as I trusted them and wasn't afraid, they would say anything to offend or hurt me or be thinking negatively about me. What I'm meaning is that because they loved me, I was reassured they wouldn't intentionally do anything to harm me. The Bible says, 'There is no fear in love. But perfect love drives out fear.' *(1 John 4:18)*. Focusing on how much I'm loved by God, and dwelling on it, transformed my mind. I now find it easier not to care about what others think of me or say about me. Being right with God is what counts. He knows all and sees all as well as what is in my heart.

Two Christians, while praying for me on two separate occasions, saw a picture of a flower in bud that opened up very slowly. They told me this meant that God was going to give me confidence gradually. At that time, I was also praying for myself for confidence and boldness. God has improved my confidence tremendously. God also reduced my anxiety slowly over a two-year period. Even though I can feel uncomfortable, it's wonderful that I don't get any anxiety during social situations now.

I met my husband at church in Middlesbrough in January 2005. He's an answer to prayer, a gift from God. Until two months before my wedding on the 21st of October 2006, I had a phobia about being the centre of attention and walking down the aisle in front of everyone. I was absolutely dreading the day. As someone suggested, I'd even planned to stand at the front of the Church behind a screen and come out with my back to everyone. It's the only way I thought I could go through with it. Every time I talked about getting married or thought about it too much, it brought the fear to the surface and I burst into tears. I prayed to God a lot during this time. God showed me that it was a fear of people that was linked to my past. God then over time, slowly and gradually released all the pain that was deep inside me and eventually my fear completely disappeared. God had set me free. I could then start looking forward to my wedding day and was able to enjoy it and walk boldly down the aisle in confidence with my dad at my side.

Suffering anxiety can cause us to feel a sense of guilt or failure when the Bible tells us not to be anxious about anything. Anxiety is more than worry but it involves worrying about the future that something bad will happen. In a nutshell it's not having trust that God will take care of us. The way I looked at it was that God hasn't stopped things going wrong in the past so why should He this time.

Colin recently shared with me his reason for not getting the COVID vaccine telling me he feels that God will take care of him. I told him that God doesn't prevent us from catching a cold and Pastor caught COVID. His reply was, "God got him through though, didn't He?" Even though I believe there are two arguments to the vaccine debate that was a light bulb moment for me. I realised that God might not prevent suffering but He will see us through even if it means strengthening us to endure it. Suffering has caused me to lean more on God.

Prayer doesn't always make anything go away just as it doesn't always remove the symptoms of physical illness. Sometimes medical intervention or therapy is required. Most of us probably wouldn't think twice about taking a pill for diabetes for example so why not for anxiety if that's what it takes. However, pills don't always mean we are symptom free. All-consuming anxiety can prevent us from being able to pray. That's when we need God's grace and the prayers of others or to just pray short arrow prayers such as "please help."

During the COVID pandemic because it was new situation it would have been easy to live in fear. However, I took on board the scripture, '*let not your hearts be troubled neither let it be afraid*' (John

14;27), thus preventing fear from entering my heart. I shifted my focus and got into God's Word. I stopped watching the news so I wasn't filling my mind with all the negative reports and rising figures of people dying. I refused to partner with fear. We didn't over buy and stock up like many others were due to them being in fear of lack (not having enough). I trusted in God that we would have what we needed. *'The lord is my shepherd; I shall not want' (Psalm 23:1). 'And my God will meet all your needs according to the riches of his glory in Christ Jesus' (Philippians 4:19).* There were two tins of tomatoes left on the shelves and toilet rolls took some finding after searching various shops but we are thankful to have small supermarkets close to where we live.

It's up to us to be disciplined and try and resist the fear that tries to consume us by turning away from it and not allowing it to take hold. Focus on the Prince of Peace. Remember we are in a spiritual battle. I understand that for some this isn't possible and that fear can easily consume and take hold like it had previously for me.

My parents were close to their friend caring for him after he became ill and diagnosed by the GP, over the phone, with a chest infection. He asked them to phone the ambulance as he was unable to breathe. He was admitted to hospital straight away, diagnosed with COVID and passed away the next day. Due to my parents being in contact with him they had to isolate in the house for two weeks. We were all sure my parents would have the virus, especially given their age of 75, therefore I prayed in tongues daily. Praise God, they didn't have the slightest symptom of it. I believe that was an answer to prayer and it showed God's power at work.

During my breakdown for the first time in our married life I felt as if our marriage was on the rocks. It was extremely difficult for my husband to cope with me being as unwell as I was, as it would be for anyone in a similar position. He had become my support worker and carer. I kept thinking he wouldn't want to be with me anymore. It was all putting tremendous pressure on our marriage and creating distance between us. He was at home with me constantly, sacrificing holidays that he'd planned. But because of Jesus he always prayed and lived in hope that things would get better. I had strong faith that God could restore our marriage so when I started getting better and was able to pray, I prayed daily (as did my mum) that things would improve. God restored our marriage and it became better than ever.

Foot

In 2017 I happened to break my foot, rushing to get to church, would you believe! I'd stopped setting the alarm for church as I always woke up early. However, this particular Sunday I woke up, looked at the clock, said "it's 9.45 am," rushed out of bed, got dressed and ran down the stairs, missed the bottom step and fell in a heap at the bottom.

I consequently, never made it to church, but ended up in A&E instead. I was unable to walk but was just hoping it was only badly sprained. I was very anxious about the outcome and memories were haunting me from the bad experiences I had when I broke my wrist several years earlier. Being squeamish never helps in these situations either. The anxiety made me shake a lot and cry. I remember I kept saying to my husband, "I'm frightened". Fear had taken a hold. It was all consuming I didn't even think past it to even pray, until later when the anxiety struck again after I'd got home. My husband was very good, his presence and words of, "Don't worry, it's alright", helped me to get through it. When I look back now, it was as if Jesus was speaking to me telling me not to worry, that He had it all in hand. I felt comforted.

I'd always been petrified at the thought of an operation, which didn't help the anxiety I was already feeling. As my accident had happened on a Sunday, I was given a temporary plaster up to my knee, also an appointment for the next day and told, "it's up to the consultant whether you will have an operation". Each time the anxiety occurred at home, I was able to command the spirit of fear to go, thinking about Jesus on the cross and asking for his peace.

I attended the appointment with the consultant the next day. People were now praying for me so I was calmer than I had been the day before and during the night. For those who are medically- minded the break was down the length of my fifth metatarsal bone in my right foot. It's the long bone attached to your little toe. The consultant started asking me questions regarding whether I was fit and well, my age, my job and then proceeded to talk about the bone I'd broken. The whole time I was getting more and more anxious. He could then see the fear in my face and asked me what was wrong. I said I didn't want an operation. He stated, "you aren't having an operation". The anxiety started to drain away and I couldn't thank him enough. I was that relieved I told him, "I could almost kiss you".

When I had broken my wrist a few years earlier it needed manipulating and I was told I had to cancel my holiday in case it displaced and I needed an operation. I remember going into the room where they replace your plaster and crying. She told me it wouldn't hurt. I told her I was upset because I'd just found out we had to cancel our holiday. Despite me consistently praying with all my might against an operation, as it happened, I did require the operation. I haven't got any answers as to why God didn't give me what I asked for, other than He isn't a slot machine, but I can honestly say that being in hospital turned out to be an absolute blessing.

What helped me was talking to others with similar injuries and reaching out to a couple of elderly women there. One lady had dementia and I loved being there for her, as she was the one who didn't get the visitors. All I can say is that I just loved being there and didn't want to go home. It was as if Jesus had used this to provide me with the emotional healing that I needed. And to look at my wrist now you wouldn't know it had ever been broken. It works just as it did before the break and I don't have any pain. I give all the praise to God for providing me with what I needed and the best consultant as he did a marvelous job.

Something I noticed through all the experience with my foot, was that I experienced a reduction in my stomach pains. I realised that it wasn't only my job that could be causing stress but the entire business of life when working, and I'm also aware that my hearing problems cause me quite a bit of stress at work. This may not make sense to others but it was refreshing to have a break from always being focused on my IBS. The situation diverted my mind, especially during the first two weeks. In between the times of struggling, I had a great sense of relaxation and peacefulness.

After the initial shock of breaking my foot, I started to enjoy this time I had to relax. I then began to start thinking about Psalm 23:2-4 where it says, *'He makes me lie down in green pastures, he leads me beside quiet waters. He restores my soul.'* Our soul consists of our mind, will and emotions. It proved to be a time of refreshing and renewal. One's working life can be very draining, causing frustration and stress with everything else that needs doing, especially when living with health problems. As I wasn't able to do a lot I was forced to rest.

I hadn't appreciated how exhausting it could be having a broken foot. After I'd cooked tea, I was exhausted and after I'd got up and dressed, I was exhausted. Everything took so much effort and extra energy. My leg muscles and feet needed to rest due to them aching. My foot needed rest and elevation to reduce the swelling. When I felt up to it, I was hoping I'd be able to paint some of the fence. However, it happened to rain just about every day for three weeks, in-between the periods of sun. I kept thinking, "God doesn't want me to do that fence". God certainly made me lie back and put my feet up. I enjoyed just laying on my beautifully soft recliner in the garden just looking at flowers and observing the bees and butterflies. God forced me to notice the beauty of his creation in a way that I didn't usually do. This was another time when I experienced Him bringing good out of a bad situation. I was given the time of restoration, refreshment, renewal and replenishment that my body and mind required. It felt so good as I wasn't usually able to attain this.

While it was on my mind that I had an appointment to go back to hospital on 31st July and thinking about the fact that I may be anxious again, God gave me the exact scripture I needed for how I was feeling. *Don't be afraid, for I am with you. Don't be discouraged, for I am your God. I will strengthen you and help you. I will hold you up with my victorious right hand' Isaiah 41:10). NLT*

One day whilst reading my daily devotional, The Daily Bread, it made me think about the overwhelming fear I'd experienced. It was titled "I'm Really Scared…". The scripture was, *'For I am your God who takes hold of your right hand and says to you; Do not fear; I will help you.'* Because we can't always feel His presence, we often tend to forget that God is right there with us in all our trials, struggles and difficulties and remembering this helps us to have hope.

A couple of days later I was reading my Psalm 63 when verses 6-8 spoke to me, *"Because you are my helper, I sing for joy in the shadow of your wings. I cling to you; your strong right hand holds me securely."* God wanted me to know that he was holding my right hand with His. I visualised him doing this when I felt anxious at my next hospital appointment.

I experienced anxiety at different points on my journey, whilst getting my cast removed and after symptoms and bad pain flared due to the exercises. It was appearing that it was impossible to pray off the anxiety as it kept resurfacing each time the pain and symptoms got worse and disappearing when the symptoms calmed down. I spoke to people I knew involved in healing ministry and a lady came to pray with me. We established the anxiety was something that occurred in the generational line.

Therefore, I said the necessary prayers and the lady prayed for me. At the time I didn't feel any different so wasn't convinced I was set free. However, since that day even though I unfortunately ended up doing more damage to my foot the anxiety didn't return. God is just amazing! It's times like this that I'm overwhelmed with gratitude that He is in my life.

One thing we don't tend to think about too much is the trauma that can be involved in any accident. Two weeks after my accident I attended one of the teaching sessions I'd been involved in, which just happened to be on accident and trauma. I was asked if I'd had prayer for the trauma, which is something I hadn't even considered. Shock can have a big impact on our bodies and emotions, which I realised could have also contributed to my anxiety. They prayed for me, prayed off the trauma and also against the fear I'd been experiencing. I was told to repent of the fear and ask Jesus's forgiveness for not trusting in Him. Since then, I feel blessed to be able to say I didn't experience the effects of the trauma any more.

Ten weeks after my accident one of the Elders at church said he woke up with pain in the sole of his feet and ankles, which is exactly where my pain was at the time. He made an announcement for anyone to go forward for prayer who had foot pain. I made it to the front with just one crutch but had gone in using the two. Since then, the symptoms got worse, but from the Wednesday I noticed things seemed to be gradually improving and I no longer required the crutches. However, I did take the crutches to my physiotherapy appointment on the Thursday as I hadn't walked any distance outside. I got a wonderful two minute massage to which I was amazed got me walking more freely. I was given exercises to get a fuller range of movement in my foot. A few days later I then felt able to start learning to go downstairs properly rather than sideways as I had been up till then.

As I've already mentioned, God brings good out of bad situations and whilst on the sick (due to my foot) from work, I couldn't remember the last time I had felt so well in my body as well as my mind. I was not experiencing any aches and pains in my arms and legs as I usually did, apart from what was related to my injury or as a result of using the crutches. It made me realise that if I did go back to work, I needed to think and pray about not only managing my stress but my time as well and stop rushing about to get things done. The only way to do this was to ask God to help me. My foot had caused me to slow down, which wasn't a bad thing. I know that in the natural state of affairs at work, I could never achieve the wellbeing I had whilst on the sick. Work had its own stresses that there was no getting away from.

However, when I didn't get made redundant with some of the others, I knew that God wanted me in that job. Therefore, I prayed again, telling God my concerns and leaving it in His hands. As I've said before, God knows best. He knows what's right for

us more than we do. If I found that my foot
problems meant I was unable to manage the job, I
felt peace in the fact that my job didn't define who I
was. God will have us where we can be best used
for Him, even if it may not always be an easy place
for us to be. However, I did manage to get back to
work, even though I wasn't able to walk far at first,
and over time God completely healed my foot. One
of the most exciting things was how God was
constantly using me at work with the clients I
supported. It confirmed I was in the place where
God wanted me.

Lucky

During the time of my immense stress when I was
trying to get used to using my hearing aids, my cat
Lucky, who was nineteen years old, became ill. The
vets struggled to know what the problem was. He
wasn't eating and started pacing up and down the
settee crying out, as if he was suffering anxiety. It
wasn't known whether he was in pain. Therefore,
after some thought and prayer, we made a decision
for him to be put to sleep, brought him home and
buried him in our garden. Anyone, who has ever
had a family pet put to sleep, will understand how
difficult and upsetting this can be. It was a big loss
to both of us, but especially to me, as the cat had
been such a special part of my life for nineteen
years. Myself and others prayed for God's help to
get us through the grief.

One day, when I came home from work, a couple of days after his passing, I opened the front door and a grey and white cat ran straight into the house. I'd seen her before but not for a long time. She would turn up at two or three day intervals and I was sure that God had sent her to comfort me. This lifted me up so much that even though she stopped coming as often, a week didn't go by without her coming to visit us. She was an immense blessing to both of us. We left biscuits and water out for her. It appeared she sometimes just visited to have a long comfy sleep and goodness me she slept for England. We often joked about how great it was to have a part time lodger. It's a bit like grandparents who say that it's lovely to have the grandchildren visit, and it's lovely when they go back. She was absolutely adorable, and we loved her to bits. I don't know how many names she had as my husband named her 'Bonny' and the kids over the road, who she also visited, named her 'Sparkle'. God most definitely used this cat to heal my pain.

However, sadly, during 2016, whilst I was writing this book, we received some terrible news that our little visitor had died. One of the ladies over the road found her ill on their drive and after taking her to the vets learnt, that not only was she in fact was a he, but that he'd been poisoned by some anti-freeze. I don't know whether this was deliberate or not, but it left me very upset, as you can imagine. After the trauma of losing Lucky, we'd decided not to get another cat of our own.

Emotional Healing

Emotional health is different to mental health in that mental health involves our decision making and interaction with others where as emotional health involves our feelings and one's ability to manage emotions.

Things that take our minds off ourselves and our health can produce healing by maintaining mental wellbeing. I've found this to be the case when interceding (praying for others), which, being a compassionate person, I've been naturally drawn to do. When others' problems are worse than your own, it also helps put yours in perspective and not seem as bad.

I remember a sermon being preached once, where it was explained that the next time you feel under pressure, take your eyes off yourself and pray for someone else. Then, within half an hour, you'll have victory over Satan. *'The prayer of a righteous person is powerful and effective.'* (James 5:16).

Emotional healing can result from being understood by others, who offer comfort. It can help us manage our emotions. I heard a speaker at 'Aglow' (women's meetings), who gave her testimony. I was amazed that she had been through what I was going through with my chemical sensitivity such a rare illness, that you seldom come across anyone else who has had it. I cried all the way through her testimony, because I could relate to what she was saying. I was so grateful to meet someone in person, who had been through a similar experience. Rebecca became a good source of encouragement to me over the following few years. At Aglow she shared how the song 'You Raise Me Up' had ministered to her during her times of ill health. This was exactly the same song that had ministered to me. Years after receiving my healing I met another lady, who had chemical sensitivity. She attended the same church as my mum. I was then able to reach out to her and gave her a chemical sensitivity devotional book to help her.

I became aware, that negative emotions such as bitterness, guilt and anger have deep roots and can contribute to ill health and disease. Partly for this reason, I had help with releasing these emotions through 'Inner Healing' from a couple who carried out this kind of work voluntarily, out of the goodness of their hearts. It involved talking over past life events, then healing the memories through prayer by letting the Holy Spirit direct and guide the sessions. All of us are affected by our past in negative ways and as a result, carry negative feelings that we might not even be aware of. But God is in the business of healing hearts. I was healed of inner pain that I felt was not helping my physical health problems. Since being a Christian, as I began to feel valued and loved by God, I've been healed and set free from feelings of inferiority, rejection, insecurity, not being good enough, feeling unlovable, and low self-esteem. God has also used movies to play a big part in my healing, as inner pain was again released when I related to something in the movie, that connected to something in my past.

There were days when I believed I couldn't do what it took, such as adhering to my restricted diet, going to work when feeling unwell or fatigued or not knowing whether I was going to be sick whilst there. I regularly thought that it was too much, and I was too sick to carry on. Such negative thoughts keep us down.

How we feel can be a choice. It hasn't been easy to do but by praising and thanking God and by reading and speaking out scriptures it has helped control my negative feelings. This has enabled me to feel better about things and gave me some hope. Praising God has the power to change our hearts and our thoughts.

I believe we need peace about our circumstances, no matter what they are, as a lack of peace in your mind and heart can make you miserable. Sickness can steal your peace. Jesus died so that we could have peace and he is much bigger than our circumstances. I understand that at times sickness steals our peace. However, reminding ourselves of

God's goodness can keep us hopeful and bring us peace.

God gave me many words and scriptures that spoke to me throughout this difficult time. One was what a friend gave me from a little book called 'Divine Help For Today's Needs' by Fr. John Woolley which reads,

'PEACE My child, let my peace enfold you… not looking at yourself but at Me! Consciously and frequently rest your spirit in that peace; it brings true healing, and is all that you need.

Eagerly desire My peace for its uniqueness; know that it neutralises long standing hurts. Unless My peace works upon deep wounds, you are at the mercy from the past-its pain revived.

Firmly refuse unloving ways, wrong ways, which would temporarily destroy My peace in you; refuse them in My strength. Do not 'analyse' whether you have My peace; just know that it is there, as you are careful to tread My way… and it will pass from you to My other children.

My name -the Name of JESUS -brings peace; Say it to Me-in love; say it to yourself -to comfort your heart, unfailing.

'Do not let your heart be troubled, or afraid'. (John 14:27).

Words like these totally comforted me, giving me more strength to carry on. I rested in that peace as it said, which healed my heart. I was learning to allow his love, joy and peace to fill me no matter how I felt.

As suggested in Freedom in Christ, I made myself a little Spiritual First Aid Box to use at times when I'm struggling with negative thoughts, feelings and emotions. It contains two 'Our Daily Bread' booklets 'Hope and Strength in Times of Illness' and 'Comfort For When Life Hurts,' which both include daily devotions. 'The Father's Love Letter', one of Penny's poems, a booklet containing scriptures of healings that Jesus performed, to raise my faith. I've included a list of things to help get me through, such as Psalms and reminders of uplifting and helpful things to read and pray. I've also included a reminder to read some post it notes I've kept from courses with all the nice things on that people have said about me, to remind me of my positive qualities. This little box is useful as it is difficult during times when we are feeling low, stressed or anxious to recall to mind what can help. The challenge is remembering to use it when difficulties occur. A scrap book I keep full of funny animal clippings is also a helpful thing to look at during times of stress.

Sometimes God needs to minister to emotional healing before physical healing can take place. Often when I had prayer for my physical health, inner pain was released. Healing often needs to happen on the inside within our mind, before we can ever have a chance of being fully healed on the outside. The trouble is life throws more and more things at us that can cause more emotional pain, often requiring healing to be an ongoing process.

Physical Healing

I'm so glad I've kept a record and written down the things that God has said to me over the years. At the Church home group that I was part of in 2009, they were praying for my healing from the chemical sensitivity, when Amy, who ran it, got this scripture; *'The LORD your God is with you, the Mighty Warrior who saves. He will take great delight in you; in his love he will no longer rebuke you, but will rejoice over you with singing.'* *(Zephaniah 3:17).* Ten days later I randomly picked out a scripture from our promise box and got the same passage. I believe that this confirmed that God was speaking to me. God's Word can be so encouraging and uplifting, particularly when He speaks right into your situation as He did for me. A couple of weeks later Amy wrote something down for me that Joyce Meyer has said to speak out, that is 'I'm getting better and better every day in every way.' Amy told me to say this whilst looking in the mirror. I practiced this daily. I believe this helped raise my hope and faith for healing. What we speak it out often enough, we come to believe it.

The first Church we attended after moving to Darlington in 2008 was called Xcell. There I met a lady called Angelina, who informed me about some food supplements she was taking, that had helped improve her health. As they were fairly expensive to buy and I had already wasted my money so many times in the past in my search to find a cure or just some improvement, I decided to pray about it. I was finally learning to take things to God first. I must have prayed for about a year before I felt it was right to try them. The supplements were vitamins, minerals and antioxidants. I decided to try one month's supply at first, which made me feel much better. I was soon fully cured from all the nasty symptoms of chemical sensitivity I was experiencing and have been taking them at a reduced dose ever since. I believe that God can use anything to bring healing, some of these being medication and supplements, but again we have to be discerning about what to take and who to believe. It's thought that in those who have chemical sensitivity their detox system isn't functioning correctly to detox chemicals out fast enough. This would explain why the supplements worked.

The scripture, that spoke to me and comforted me the most during times of intense fatigue, was '*But those who hope in the LORD will renew their strength. They will soar on wings like eagles; they will run and not grow weary, they will walk and not be faint,*' (Isaiah 40:31). I stood on this promise. In time I received the healing I was asking for. I can thankfully say, I reached a place where I could run and not grow weary, I could walk and not be faint.

I'm not talking about a running a marathon here but just maybe running to catch a bus. I could walk to work, which took about thirty to forty minutes. without feeling weak and weary. When I realised that I could do things I couldn't before, I then know that God had brought some healing to my body, and that is the best feeling ever.

One day I was just happily walking when I suddenly went over on my ankle. I somehow managed to hobble home but it was extremely painful and quickly swelled up to the size of a golf ball even though I kept placing frozen peas on it. Therefore, I panicked I'd done some serious damage and really didn't want to go to hospital, having to undergo x rays and appointments again. In the heat of anxiety and horrendous pain I phoned two friends. When panic prevents us from thinking straight, we need the wisdom of others. My Christian friend told me I needed help and that Jesus would help me. My other friend suggested I phone 111, which I did who told me to wait for a call back which came several hours later from a Paramedic. She asked me several questions and I breathed a sigh of relief when she informed me, I could treat it at home and there was no need to attend hospital. At this point the anxiety started draining away.

With the amount of foot problems, I'd previously encountered I felt as if I'd earned a degree in foot healing. This time rather than rest it I knew to walk on it as much as I could in order to strengthen it.

Therefore, after two days on crutches, as the pain prevented me from walking on it, that's what I did. Even though I had a collection of muscle rubs, including one I'd made myself with coconut oil and essential oils, I was still expecting a long healing process. A friend went to collect a prescription for me and asked if that's all there was. I told her I ordered some gel as well but it wasn't urgent as I had enough. She replied, "if you haven't, you'll make some." We had a laugh about it.

Whilst praying over my foot the Holy Spirit brought to my mind the 'balm of Gilead' mentioned in the Bible. This gave me so much reassurance as it was confirmation that Jesus was looking after me. I didn't know anything about it, so I googled it and learned it has deep tissue healing properties reducing pain and inflammation and speeding healing. My friend stated that if God recommends it to people it's got to be good stuff. Very true I thought. I felt He was wanting me to apply it spiritually so I did that every day to find it started to heal quickly.

'I actually happened to purchase some balm of Gilead online but when it arrived and I found out it had been prayed over with the wrong spirit my instant thought was that I couldn't possibly use it. Therefore, I sent the following message to the seller who was ever so nice about it telling me to post it back for a refund. 'I'm very disappointed in receiving this oil. I ordered in faith as its mentioned in the Bible. I later read that it has been prayed over with another spirit other than the Holy Spirit. I'm sorry but I can't possibly use this oil I bought in faith for my sprained ankle. I hope you understand me as a Christian and appreciate my faith. I've ordered this by mistake as it said it was a pure organic oil. I apologise for my error. Will you kindly refund me please.' They agreed to refund me straight away. Sometimes God uses situations like this to witness to others.

Freedom in Christ

Whilst on my sick leave from work (as a result of bullying) I bumped into two lovely Christian ladies I know called Maureen and Thelma, who could see how I was suffering and offered to take me through 'The Freedom in Christ' course. It's about how to overcome our fight with the world, the flesh and the Devil. It teaches us how to fulfil this scripture '*We demolish arguments and every pretension that sets itself up against the knowledge of God, and we take captive every thought to make it obedient to Christ,' (2 Corinthians 10:5)*. We do this by managing our thoughts and refusing some of them to enter our minds. It's easy to speak negatively about our pain, discomfort, weaknesses, health concerns or difficult situations. The more we concentrate on the problem, the more that problem consumes us. This works in the same way as CBT (cognitive behavioural therapy) does.

What we allow our minds to dwell on is our choice. Our emotions are generated by our thoughts, they come from how we interpret life. To rid ourselves of negative emotions we must learn to change the way we think. The goal is to renew our mind by having more faith in the truth of God's Word, rather than sticking to what we see, feel or think. *'Be transformed by the renewing of your mind.' (Romans 12:2)*. Rejecting negative thoughts and combatting them with the truth of God's Word sets us free from all the negative thoughts and feelings we're having so we can start to believe all the positive things that God thinks and says about us. God's Word is a sword to use in spiritual warfare to come against negative thoughts.

The enemy can try to make us believe lies about ourselves that make us feel worthless etc., but we can choose to believe what God says about us in His Word. It's about focusing on fact (the truth of God's Word) rather than our feelings, which can often lie to us. We believe in our heart what we speak out and it's healthier to speak the truth that's in God's Word.

We need to be selective about what we believe about ourselves. As Joyce Meyer says, the mind is a battlefield! God says we are loved, accepted, adopted as His child, chosen, God's workmanship, fearfully and wonderfully made, to name but a few. *'Above all else, guard your heart, for everything you do flows from it,' (Proverbs 4:23)*. We guard our hearts by capturing any thoughts that aren't in

line with God's Word, before they have chance to
enter.

These two lovely ladies, as much as the course,
were an enormous blessing and help to me. The
Freedom in Christ course helped me in many ways,
including forgiving more deeply and seeing people
through Jesus's eyes, as they were lost souls going
to hell. When they were praying for me, Maureen
felt that God wanted me to not look at myself and
how I was feeling too much but look at the bigger
picture through my work situation and what God
was doing. This really helped me to refocus my
mind, as it wasn't about me. I wasn't fully aware
what God was doing but we are all witnesses for
Christ and people see how we behave differently to
none Christians and cope differently in situations.

I had so much support from others who stood
alongside me and prayed for me. My dad, who isn't
a Christian, has also always given me great words
of wisdom and encouragement through times when
my health was at its worst. God spoke through
people to lift me up and strengthen me.

Building Character

Jesus is our example. *'Then they hurled their insults
at him, he did not retaliate; when he suffered, he
made no threats. Instead, he entrusted himself to
him who judges justly,' (1 Peter 2:23).* As the Bible
states, if we leave insults against us in God's hands,

He will deal with those people in the right way. Therefore, we do not take revenge but trust in God.

I believe God allowed me being bullied at work in order to teach me several things. I'm generally an honest open person, but it taught me to be wiser, watching what I shared and with whom, as innocent things I had said or done had been used against me. God said in His Word '*I am sending you out like sheep among wolves. Therefore, be as shrewd as snakes and as innocent as doves.*' *(Matt 10:16)*. I felt like a lamb amongst wolves, ready to be pounced on by my colleagues at every opportunity, who would use whatever they could against me. This statement helped me at the time; 'It doesn't matter how many people have tried to knock you down, praise God for allowing them to see you're still standing!' Because I obeyed Gods commands, I didn't have any resentment, bitterness or ill feelings towards those colleagues.

God took me by surprise when he set me free from something that had been stopping me from being the person that He wanted me to be, something that had pressed me down, all my life. I'd received a word from God, through someone who prayed for me, during a New Wine Summer Camp. They stated that God was going to break down my timidity. This came to pass during my difficulties at work (bullying), evident in the fact that I stood up for myself by questioning and challenging my ill treatment, something I'd always found too difficult to do. It was only with God's help and grace that I managed to persevere and not give up. *'I can do all this through him (Christ) who gives me strength.' (Philippians 4:13).* His promises were in my life. At times when I didn't have the answers, I left it with God knowing he had all the answers and would sort it all out for me. In Romans it states that all things work together for good. God never let me down, He was always there to fight for me. *'The LORD will fight for you; you need only to be still.' (Exodus 14:14).*

With me being such an emotional person, I prayed for God to strengthen my heart and my emotions and I could see Him doing this gradually. Sometimes something said or done to us can wound and hurt us as it relates to a past experience, maybe in our childhood. that hasn't been dealt with and healed. This strengthening has served me well in my current job as a community support worker working with vulnerable people, as I've dealt with many challenging situations, such as angry clients, without it upsetting me as it had done previously.

I was amazed at how God gave me everything I needed for that situation, including strength and determination that I never knew could be possible, just as God promised He will in *Philippians 4:19*; *'...and my God will meet all your needs according to the riches of his glory in Christ Jesus.'* Even though it knocked my confidence I stayed secure in who I was as a person in Christ. God needed to take me out of the work situation for a while to strengthen me, heal me and build me up, ready to go back to work and continue to fight the battle; the battle of spiritual warfare.

People of the world often gain their self worth from selfish ambition and lust for power. However, my worth isn't defined by anything the world can offer or what human people say or think about me. My worth is in what God says and thinks about me. *'I praise you because I am fearfully and wonderfully made; your works are wonderful; I know that full well.' (Psalm 139:14).* When you know who you are in Christ it changes how you think and feel about yourself. My security and self worth wasn't dependent on my colleagues' acceptance. Even though I wasn't accepted at work, I was sure I was accepted, secure and significant in Christ Jesus, according to what His Word says about me. I knew that I was chosen, well loved, blessed, precious, a child of God. *'For I am convinced that neither death nor life, neither angels nor demons, neither the present nor the future, nor any powers, neither height nor depth, nor anything else in all creation, will be able to separate us from the love of God that is in Christ Jesus our Lord' (Romans 8:38-39).* The healing comforting love that God showed me through others' support, at this time, was absolutely amazing. I still had a lot going for me, I was sure of that and even though my confidence had been affected, my self-esteem remained strong, because of Christ.

Your mind can tell you that you are no good and make you feel worthless with negative thoughts.

Everyone is important and each person brings things to the world that no one else can. Declarations I've used were;

- I'm important and I matter
- I'm more than a conqueror
- I am an overcomer
- I'm deeply loved and cherished by my Heavenly Father
- I am a 'warrior'
- I love and accept myself (something I've had to work on over the years and only achieved since being a Christian)
- I am chosen and highly favoured

Neuroscientific studies show that self affirmations like these have been shown to decrease health deteriorating stress (Sherman et al, 2009; Critcher & Dunning, 2015).

Revelations

Speaking Gods Word out as I've described earlier in the book, didn't seem to be showing any evidence of having a positive effect on my physical healing, except for helping me to be more positive and hopeful. However, I later read that what we believe and speak whether positive or negative has a similar effect on our immune system. *'Death and life are in the power of the tongue: and they that love it shall eat the fruit thereof' (Proverbs 18:21, KJV)* For example, there has been research showing that cancer patients with a positive outlook are generally more likely to live longer. This is where Christian faith can help. I heard of an incident where someone was told they had cancer and died a few weeks ago as the thought of dying consumed them, but it was later revealed that it was all a mistake and he didn't in fact have cancer at all. The mind is very powerful.

It just shows what can be going on in our bodies without us being aware of it. God's Word is positive and filled with love so therefore, this was probably helping to improve my immune system. Changes whether positive or negative can be so subtle and gradual that they are not noticeable.

God's Word is stated in Proverbs 4:22 as being medicine to all our flesh. I took the Word like you would medicine, speaking it out into my inner being two or three times daily. I realised that when speaking out scriptures it's also a case of believing they are true.

In Mark 5:25-28 a woman with an issue of blood said, *'if I may touch his (Jesus') clothes, I shall be made whole'*. She spoke these words out in faith, even though she didn't feel well. Her words penetrated her spirit and she began to see herself well. *'Faith is the confidence that what we hope for will actually happen; it gives us assurance about things we cannot see.' (Hebrews 1:11)*. Her hope was to be healed, but faith gave confidence to her hope and caused healing to be manifested in her body. It's about calling those things into being that don't exist. *'God who gives life to the dead and calls into being things that were no.' (Romans 4:17).*

Confessing the Word builds up our faith, which then gives us hope. But we have to remember to always focus on the fact that Jesus is our healer and not our confessing or our hope or anything else, even though these are contributing factor.

I read about a lady who had a long term auto immune disease and confessed healing scriptures for one year. During that time her symptoms got worse. The enemy will do anything to make us doubt our faith and believe it isn't working. But she kept confessing God's Word and after one year she was totally healed and was still healed years later. The same happened to me when I took communion daily. My symptoms worsened. It can be one of the enemy's tactics to prevent us from being healed. If we stop doing what we are doing due to our health worsening then we won't encounter our breakthrough and will miss out on our chance of healing.

At one stage I stopped going on long walks of more than an hour due to the resulting pain in my legs and back and the accompanying exhaustion. When on holiday, I'd be ill with all the walking, not being one for just sitting but wanting to see the sights. Years ago, I remember my husband innocently commenting, "You're going to be in a wheelchair". Just one comment like this can have a negative effect for years if we choose to accept it. People who make negative remarks like these are in effect putting a curse on us. If anyone speaks anything negative over me now, I refuse to accept it and pray it off straight away. We can also speak negative words over ourselves. But for every negative word or statement spoken, there is always a positive scripture to be found to come against it. For example:

I can't do it. *I can do all things through Christ who strengthens me. Philippians 4:13*
I am afraid. *God has not given me a spirit of fear, but of power, love and a sound mind. 2 Timothy1:7*

It's a challenge not to say negative things as we all do it, at times without us even being aware of what we've said. But there are times when we need to speak things out to express how we feel, sometimes to others and mostly to God, as David did in the Psalms.

One particular day when I'd been struggling very badly with quite severe medication withdrawal symptoms, a prophecy and prayer invitation popped up on Facebook that I felt God wanted me to attend via zoom. My husband said, 'you are like a' I finished his sentence with 'a dying swan'. But it proved to be beneficial. They listened to God and then a lady asked if I had neck pain, which I told her I did, so they prayed for that. Then others told me what they heard the Holy Spirit say, which was very encouraging. One man told me that I've got the oil of joy. He said, "Joy is a weapon that puts you above your enemies" and reminded me of the scripture *'The joy of the Lord is your strength'* *(Nehemiah 8:10).*

I remember listening to some Christian teaching that talked about us all having joy within us but sometimes that joy needs to be cultivated. They said on down days we need things that cause our joy to rise, which are different for everyone. For example, play worship songs, read particular books, watch a film, speak Bible verses. Whatever works for you.

The ministry team on zoom then asked what I wanted prayer for so I explained about withdrawing from mirtazapine. Afterwards the lady who prayed informed me that she was helping her dad come off mirtazapine and that I need to take it slowly. It's just fabulous how God knows what we need and put me in touch with someone who can understand how difficult it is.

A lovely lady I met sent me a message which said, 'I've heard it's a really hard drug to come off. You're really brave I've lots of respect for you. God bless you, 'Sleep well xx'. I messaged back to thank her and let her know that meant a lot to me. I feel we don't always reach out to others like God wants us to. An encouraging text or a message letting someone know we are thinking of them or praying for them can really lift that person up.

As I've said I didn't use to like the quiet, gentle nature that God had given me. I wished that I could be much more confident and outspoken. Several times people, who had never met me before, prayed for me and told me that God loves my gentleness. This had a profound and positive impact on the way I saw myself. Finding this scripture was a revelation, *'Rather, it should be that of your inner self, the unfading beauty of a gentle and quiet spirit, which is of great worth in God's sight.' (1 Peter 3:4).* People who are healthy and strong don't usually need gentleness. However, when a person is weak and hurting gentleness is a quality that's much needed in order to touch and heal them

In 2013, when I was extremely ill with a virus and not knowing what the future would hold with my gut pain, God spoke to me. He said, *"I need you to go through this because I am going to use you to reach out to the sick, to minister to the sick. They (the sick) will flock to you like birds to a nest.*
You will be their comfort, their strength, their hope in times of trouble.
In times when they have no hope, you'll be their encourager.
And in that you will show them Me.
You'll be a carrier of My presence, my light, my love and bring people to know Me.
I am the God who heals, the Holy one of Egypt, your comforter, your strength.
The all-consuming fire.
My radiance and all that I am will flow through you like rivers of living water, which brings life.

Have hope because I have given you hope."

I have reached out to sick people and been able to relate to and identify with what they were going through. Moreover, four years after I had the virus, I was able to attend some Healing Ministry and Healing and Deliverance Ministry teaching sessions that were being run in Darlington for the first time. Christians usually have to travel a long distance from Darlington in order to get this teaching. It's what God put on my heart even without any memory of the above word. The teaching enabled me to understand healing more in depth from a Christian perspective and all the experience I have with the people I support and different problems I deal with in in my job has helped dramatically. I feel as if God had already been training me up for the work, He is preparing me to do. *'For we are God's handiwork, created in Christ Jesus to do good works, which God prepared in advance for us to do' (Ephesians 2:10).* He has a plan and purpose for each and every one of us.

During one period of depression, I got a word from a Christian who said, "the enemy is using your illness to hold you back." I knew that I was being held back, but didn't associate it with being the enemy. When this was revealed to me, I was able to pray against it. If we aren't aware something negative is happening to us, we can't do anything to help ourselves, which was the place I was in for some time. The enemy can be our biggest deceiver. When we are in such a bad place, whether that be stress, depression or a really difficult situation, we often need people to point out to us what might otherwise have been obvious to us. We need encouragement from others. In 1 Thessalonians 5:11 it states, *'Therefore encourage one another and build each other up, just as in fact you are doing'*.

Prayer has played a big part in all my searching, as I prayed for God to show me the way forward, reveal things to me and show me the way to go. Choosing an attitude of thanksgiving, praise and trust is a must in any Christians life as it's what scripture tells us to do. God is the God of the breakthrough. We need to be persistent in prayer and not giving up before that breakthrough. Can you imagine stopping praying just before someone is due to be healed or saved? That's why the Bible says to persevere in prayer. It's faith that enables us to keep praying when we don't see an answer. I have prayers written in my journal which I pray regularly. I have chosen two to include here that are based on scripture. The first is a useful reminder of God's goodness;

Hebrews 13:5 says, 'You will never leave me nor forsake me'. You are my helper. I declare and believe that everything will work out. You will not fail me. You will cause me to be an overcomer. I will trust in You and You will make a way. You will strengthen me for every battle, give me wisdom for every decision and peace that passes all understanding. You have me in the palm of Your hand.

The next one I chose to include is a prayer for healing;

Thank you, God, that You formed me and You knit me together. I am fearfully and wonderfully made. You know me by name. You know my inner most parts. You spoke everything into being. You spoke to the wind, the waves and the fig tree. I speak life, health and healing to my body. You spoke to the mountain and it was cast into the sea. I speak to all sickness in my body to be removed and cast out. I command my body to work and function as God created it to in Jesus' name. I claim back my peace now. Body, be relaxed, be at peace in Jesus' name. My body is blessed, strong, prosperous, favoured and healthy. Thank you that you died for me and took my sickness on the cross and by Your stripes I am healed and made whole.

In June 2020 whilst meditating on the Scripture *'I lift my eyes to the mountains (hills). Where does my help come from? My help comes from the Lord, the maker of heaven and earth (Psalm 121:1-2),* I wrote out what I heard the Holy Spirit saying to me; which is what I heard in my spirit,

God says look up!
Look to what I've got for you.
I have good things in store for you.
I love you with all my heart, with an everlasting love.
The best is yet to come!

I want good things for you.
I adore you! You are the apple of my eye, my
Princess, my Bride.
I want to bless you.
Keep looking to Me.
Acknowledge Me in everything you do.
Claim your inheritance as a child of the living God.
Be aware of My presence.
Gaze upon My beauty!

Confusion

Confusion as I've mentioned previously, can be the
result of trying to figure everything out. I've been a
person who analysed everything, which is one thing
that doing a university degree taught me. I always
wanted to find answers to everything including my
health problems and the difficulty I was in at work,
which often left me more confused. However, I
came to realise that where God is concerned you
can't work things out and He sees things differently
to us. *'For my thoughts are not your thoughts,
declares the Lord. As the heavens are higher than
the earth, so are my ways higher than your ways
and my thoughts than your thoughts' (Is. 55:8).* We
think within the scope of our human minds, as our
minds allow us to, whereas God can see everything
now and far into the future. It can be so tempting to
get involved in reasoning and trying to figure things
out as it's human instinct. There are times when
God does reveal to us what is going on but the
majority of the time, in my experience He doesn't.

This can leave us guessing and jumping to conclusions.

Sometimes for our own good it's best not to see the full picture of what is going on and what the future holds. However, during times like this I've always been comforted by the scripture in Romans 8:28 where it says, '*And we know that in all things God works for the good of those who love him, who have been called according to his purpose*'. I have kept the card on my kitchen cupboard, as a reminder, which says 'God always knows best' and I know now that this is so true. God can see things that we can't and He knows everything about us and the situations we are going through. He is in control! That's why we need to trust in Him, believing it will all work out for our good, if we keep looking to and believing in Him. One of my problems has been that I've listened to people too much in the past, often thinking that they know better, which hasn't always been the case. 'God always knows best' has involved a process of working towards this being at the forefront of my mind, as it is absolutely true. '*It is better to trust in the Lord than to put confidence in man' (Psalm 118:8, King James)*. He knows everything about us and can see into the future what we don't see.

One of my favourite scriptures is '*Trust in the Lord with all your heart and lean not on your own understanding; in all your ways acknowledge him and he will make your paths straight. Do not be wise in your own eyes, fear the Lord and shun evil.*'

(Proverbs *3:5)*. Now, I always try to listen to God first and foremost and be directed by Him and what he wants. That way, I can be reassured that I'm doing the right thing in every decision I make and every step I take. Our own personal wisdom comes from God if we are walking right with Him and being guided by Him. It says in His Word for those lacking wisdom to ask God for wisdom. '*If any of you lacks wisdom, you should ask God, who gives generously to all without finding fault, and it will be given to you' (James 1:5).* There have been so many times when God has shown me what to do whilst supporting individuals at work. The wisdom shown to me blew me away and proved to be a better way forward than what my manager would have suggested had I gone to her for advice. I'm not saying 'don't ever listen to anyone else' but I've learnt to be discerning about what others tell me and I've had a lot of good guidance from other Christians in the past.

The Bible contains so much wisdom and insight and is a good guide for life. As it says in 2 Timothy 3:16 *"All Scripture is God-breathed and is useful for teaching, rebuking, correcting and training in righteousness" (NIV). "All Scripture is inspired by God and is useful to teach us what is true and to make us realise what is wrong in our lives. It corrects us when we are wrong and teaches us to do what is right" (NLT).*

What I've learnt

The biggest mistake someone taught me was that we don't have to put on our spiritual armour as she told me she never takes it off. I then stopped putting it on which meant that I wasn't focusing on it. Therefore, in effect it lost its power as I wasn't remembering to use it. However, Ephesians 6 tells us to put it on and Gods Word is what we should always be practicing. The point of putting it on isn't because we take it off but to reaffirm it to strengthen us for the spiritual battle. The Oxford dictionary states the meaning of reaffirm as 'state again strongly' or 'confirm the validity of (something previously established).'

I will just say a little about each peace. I put them on from my head to my feet as that way I find it easier to remember.

<u>Helmet of salvation protects our mind</u>. It reminds us of our salvation that we are set free from sin and the power it has over us.

<u>Breastplate of righteousness</u> protects our heart, the seat of our emotions so that Satan can't condemn us in any way.

<u>Belt of truth</u> reminds us to focus on the Word.

<u>Sword of the spirit</u> is the Word of God. It reminds us to pray about everything. We should declare and use the Word like Jesus did against Satan when He was tempted in the wilderness (Matthew 4:1-11).

<u>Shield of faith</u>. We should lift up and release our faith in every difficult and challenging circumstance.

Shoes of peace. Having peace enables Satan to lose his power over us when he tries to upset us.

Sometimes people don't mean to give you the wrong advice, they believe what they are telling you, and that goes for the medical profession as well. People can only tell you what is in the remit of their knowledge, experience and training they have. As we all probably have, I used to put my full trust and faith in all medical professionals believing they know best. Don't get me wrong, they do a good job and I praise God for our NHS here in the UK. But experience has taught me to question everything. Sadly, doctors, who are there to help, can often make things worse. We take medication in faith, often not being informed of side effects that can cause further health problems. This was my experience with antibiotics and antidepressants. I've often come away from the doctor's feeling helpless and without hope due to GPs not having any answers, often just saying things they thought might make me feel better. After speaking to others, sadly my experience seems to be a common occurrence. Being sent away with unanswered questions and a lack of diagnosis as I was with my chemical sensitivity, can happen all too often. When feeling I was in need of another GP appointment I was left wondering if there was any point if I was only to come away disappointed again, which was often the case.

Often there are alternatives to prescription drugs, which are better for our bodies. However, we have to be very sensible in this as it all takes wisdom, research and knowledge. They can also counteract with prescribed medication. I'm part of a Facebook group where people have been forced to take healing into their own hands, due to NHS not being able to help them. They are just lay people without qualifications, but with experience and knowledge of their own healing journey. I've found there to be some really informative people who've been forced to become experts in their own health and in my experience are a lot more knowledgeable in those subjects than the medical profession.

During my times of chemical sensitivity, I read quite a bit about chemicals. I researched online, finding that chemicals contribute to all sorts of illnesses and disease including cancers. It makes sense; all these toxins weren't around years ago, and cancer wasn't around years ago as it is now. I read that with chemical sensitivity, once the chemicals build up in your system to a certain level the symptoms occur and it is probably due to a fault in some peoples' detox systems. This all made sense and things were beginning to become clear to me. It was as if my body was unable to detox the chemicals out fast enough.

The Bible *states 'The God of all comfort who comforts us in all our troubles, so that we can comfort those in any trouble with the comfort we ourselves receive from God' (2 Corinthians 1:4).* I have been able to help others with health problems by identifying with what they are going through. I understand how constant ongoing pain can drag you down, how your health can be unpredictable and you cannot always plan ahead, causing you to cancel arrangements at the last minute. I understand how we can look well but feel rotten inside, how much time ill health can take up, how frustrating it can be just to complete day to day tasks and how much longer they can take. This can then lead all sorts of emotions such as irritability, mood swings, stress, tearfulness, low mood and depression. When dealing with all of this it can be so easy to lose our joy, which is why we need to keep so close to Jesus, as He is the lifter of our heads *'But you, LORD, are a shield around me, my glory, the One who lifts my head' (Psalm 3:3).*

Having someone identify with you can be a big healer, as it is the comfort shown through this, that soothes your soul and eases the stress. I read that the best counsellors are those who have suffered the most hurts, which makes perfect sense. It's comforting to know that in a place where you feel so alone, there is someone who can identify with what you are going through. This is where the Internet can be useful with self help groups where you can post your questions, queries, share experiences and get to know people.

I've joined several health-related groups on Facebook, which have proved to be enormously helpful by sharing suggestions, ideas, research and helping to keep my spirits up. However, I've had to be careful to be wise and discerning and not just take on board everything that people are posting. I'm also careful about which groups I sign up to as with some I find there is a lot of negativity and complaining and that doesn't do anyone any good. *'Do everything without grumbling (complaining) or arguing'. (Philippians 2:14)*. I feel it's best to try and stay as positive as possible in order to achieve the best mental wellbeing. I am now also careful about how deep to go into health related research as I've already mentioned how for me it has resulted in confusion and depression.

I've found it to be all too easy to put all my focus on one health condition, that being the one that is causing the most discomfort or problems at the time and often to forget about some of the others. All of my focus had been on my IBS for such a long time when I got a revelation whilst reading about hypothyroid symptoms. I found that some of the symptoms I'd put down to IBS or food in tolerances were symptoms of hypothyroid. I then realised that unless my thyroid problem is healed, I could always have these symptoms. This made things easier for me as knowing this enabled me to relax about them a bit more. Trying to work things out ourselves can make us believe we've found the answers to only realise later that we were totally wrong, resulting in confusion again.

Diet

We need to take time to have regular meals as food gives us fuel to keep going. Our diet is important to help achieve optimum health. For eighteen years of my life, I was vegetarian. At the time I didn't realise how important it was to replace the proteins that I would have got from eating meat. I felt I was eating a healthy diet as research suggested that vegetarians could be healthier than meat eaters. My parents kept telling me I needed some meat, but I didn't think they were right and couldn't have brought myself to eat it anyway.

Several years ago, at about the age of forty, while praying for a way forward with my health, I had a strong feeling that God wanted me to eat meat. I tried a little bit but found it too difficult to persevere with it. However, God was still prompting me. Even though it proved to be a massive challenge, I made the decision to stop being vegetarian. It was then that my sister announced she had been praying for me to eat meat. I not only had the challenge of getting used to the texture and chewiness of meat but the challenge of the smell whilst cooking, learning how to cook it and know when it was ready. It was a mixture of being frustrating, but being funny at times. Over time I noticed my low immune system started to gradually improve somewhat. There was certainly something in the meat that was benefiting my body.

A friend bought me Jordan Rubin's book for my birthday. He was cured from Crohn's disease by adhering to the diet of Bible times (stone age diet). I was unable to follow the diet due to my food restrictions but have since made a real effort to cut out all the processed foods I can. I looked to eating mainly only foods that nourish my body, are healthy, and most likely to help me heal. This meant tuning in to my body and eating foods that give me the least symptoms and most energy. This has contributed to detoxing my body from things like additives and chemicals.

We then started thinking about eating organically. However, when looking in the shops, there are only so many products available within the organic range and supermarkets only stock a limited range of organic vegetables and fruit which can vary weekly. Therefore, when an allotment my husband had his name down for became available, we decided to grow only organic produce. I then found an organic vegetable stall in Darlington and after eating these along with our small amounts of produce we managed to grew, we both realised we had more energy. When I mentioned this to the stall holder he said, 'it's not only because the produce is organic but because it's fresh as with supermarket produce you don't know how long it has been on the shelf or how far it has been transported.' I remember thinking, that's a good point, because vegetables can lose nutrients the longer, they are kept after harvesting. Lots of fruit and vegetables are also antioxidants which are good for detoxing amongst other things.

During my research I found out that certain food called FODMAPS are the foods that can cause symptoms of IBS, and the list of high FODMAP foods is huge. It was years later after ordering the Monash University FODMAP booklet I found garlic and onions to be some of the worst offenders for IBS and when cutting these out I experienced a lot of pain relief. The booklet shows whether a food is low, moderate or high FODMAP. However, it's still not that simple as everyone with IBS can tolerate different amounts and there are some variations in which foods each person can tolerate. You need to find your personal level of tolerance by trial and error as everyone can be different. It just shows that if only the doctors gave this information out it would reduce suffering for so many people. Some people see this as healing when they become symptom free. However, I personally don't view having to be on a restricted diet as healing. It's a way of managing the symptoms. One has to manage restricted diets with caution as they can cause nutrient deficiencies.

Due to its complexity, my diet has been one of the biggest challenges I've had to cope with in relation to my health. I've had to be my own nutritionist in order to reduce stomach pains. After realising that certain foods were causing my pain to be worse I either stopped eating them or ate them in smaller quantities. I've struggled to eat the wind producing vegetables as well as some fruits, beans, seeds and crisps. It has sometimes been very difficult to pin point which food has caused me problems, as it may have been more than one food, amounts or time of day it was eaten, hormones or stress. I've often prayed for guidance with my diet, in knowing what to eat and what not to eat, as well as blessing food to my body before eating it.

Through research, I became aware that fruit doesn't digest very well if eaten at the same time as other food, so I now try to eat fruit one hour before and two hours after a meal. Fibre is an IBS trigger for me, as well as fat, therefore I have to limit the amount I eat at one time and in one day. Since not consuming wheat or dairy I try to balance my tolerated number of foods with eating enough calories and right fats to keep my weight up, as it can easily drop. I had one to two spoons of coconut oil in my breakfast and tried it along with half to one tablespoon of ground flaxseed. I was very nervous about trying the flaxseed, putting it off for a long time, as I was convinced it would disagree with me as I cannot tolerate many seeds. To my surprise I'm ok with it when eaten with other food. Avocados are high in good fat but I can only tolerate a quarter of one per day. I've struggled to eat nuts, as even just one handful has triggered stomach pains. I tried soaking them overnight and drying them out in the oven, since reading they can be digested better that way, and ate them after a meal. I make fruit crumble about twice a week, which I eat one or two hours after my tea and pour canned coconut milk on, which has the consistency of cream. I realised even though I still get discomfort from the apple, that I was tolerating it better than a raw apple. I have found cooked foods to be gentler on my gut than raw as they contain less fibre. Also, fruit and vegetable skins contain fibre so it's best not to eat them whenever possible. I've had to limit oats due to its fibre content. In the past I noticed when having a main meal at lunch time, especially a fatty one such as fish and chips, I had less pain at night. But due to work and other commitments, this isn't possible to carry out on a daily basis. Apparently, our digestion works better at lunch time than at tea time. Eating in the evening after my tea became an issue. I've kept food diaries in order to try and figure out the foods that weren't agreeing with me, to sometimes realise it hadn't been the food at all but was all down to stress or it being the lead up to my period. At other times there has been no explanation that I could find.

Hopefully this has given some understanding of why it has been difficult for me to explain my problems to anyone or for them to understand, as it took me years to figure all of it out myself. After praying for healing, I feel blessed that I've finally reached a place where I'm able to manage my symptoms, mainly with diet, but also by bringing in stress relief and relaxation. It's helped me to gain more hope that one day I might be fully healed, and be able to eat the foods that I thought I'd never eat again. I feel that God has helped me find these answers by directing me to the right people and information and I am truly thankful for how far I have come.

As I couldn't pin point it to one cause, I realised I've probably got several of the many things that seem to cause stomach bloating. After eating and before my period was due, my stomach bloated out as if I was pregnant. If anyone has noticed, thankfully they haven't commented. It's probably because my trousers were often a bit on the larger side, needing a belt, due to my slim figure. I have one pair of size 6 jeans that I've often needed to expand after eating, by opening the top buttons. I've heard of some people owning two sizes of clothes, a larger size to accommodate the dreaded bloat, which I'm grateful I've never needed to do.

Even when I've seemed to find the root cause to a symptom, there isn't always an easy solution. Often supplementation can be a trial and error experience, which results in wasted money if it doesn't work. I carried out the stomach acid test to find it showed I was low, but things like this often only give an indication and can only be used as a guideline. Stomach acid helps digest your food, poor digestion being one cause of bloating. Replacement acid supplements proved to be difficult to take due to the amount of stomach pain they caused me. Digestive enzymes became the next option I tried. I found it so time consuming, even researching the best brand to buy, due to some having unwanted ingredients I may react to, effectiveness, price etc. I found you can easily spend a small fortune if you don't research the best price options.

After finding out about antibiotics depleting the good bacteria in your gut as well as the bad, I always took probiotics afterwards. Probiotics are friendly bacteria. Our guts can often have the wrong balance of good and bad bacteria with the bad overtaking the good, which is called dysbiosis. I've often had to open supplement capsules and sprinkle little bits on my food, building the dosage up slowly, so my system can tolerate them, without giving me stomach pain. I found probiotics to reduce my symptoms of muscle weakness and pain but it's a challenge finding the right ones that suite me due to side effects.

An even bigger challenge came after coming off the mirtazapine causing a histamine intolerance flare which produces similar symptoms to hay fever. My symptoms can include painful acid reflux, body itching especially during the night, itchy rashes and itchy, swollen and red eyes, extremely runny nose and catarrh as well as having a stuffed-up nose. When it's bad it is torture. The doctor tried to diagnose my eye problem over the phone but thankfully I'd taken a photo when it was at its worst so he could see what it was like. He then diagnosed me with allergic conjunctivitis. I learnt that because mirtazapine contains a strong antihistamine that's why during withdrawal the body is then flooded with extra histamine. Anything taken containing anti histamine can make the situation worse so needs to be avoided. Therefore, the only way to try and manage it is to go on the low histamine diet which means only eating those foods that are lower in histamine. I'm grateful I still have a good variety of foods to eat unlike some people in third world countries.

Conclusion

God helped me overcome everything that was meant to destroy me.

If you are living with a long-term illness whether it be physical or mental remember to give yourself grace as you are fighting a difficult battle. Practice self-compassion and focus on self-care by listening to your body.

Starting each day with a positive attitude, one of gratitude and an attitude to rise above the symptoms is one of the main things that has helped me. If you look for the blessings in any situation you will find them. Jesus being my main focus upon waking, a dependency on Him and His strength has helped immensely. I thank God for my joyful spirit and optimism that has required discipline and a daily choice

I've gained several positive things from being ill such as making friends in the support groups, eating a healthier diet and reducing the toxic load on my body. I have a much deeper understanding of what it's like for those living with a chronic illness (physical and mental), which has given me a depth of empathy I would otherwise not have had. God uses us to reach out to and identify with others who are going through a similar issue, whatever that might be. This is a great privilege and an exciting calling. If I can be a blessing to others in some way and be used by God for His glory that is my biggest desire in life.

'Praise be to the God and Father of our Lord Jesus Christ, the Father of compassion and the God of all comfort, who comforts us in all our troubles, so that we can comfort those in any trouble with the comfort we ourselves receive from God' (2 Corinthians 1:3-4).

I also have a stronger strength of character that comes with enduring trials. According to the Bible God allows trials for several reasons. Trials produce perseverance, test our faith, cause us to be more Christ like, refine us and cause us to be more dependent on God.

The journey I've encountered with God through my ill health has been one amazing and awesome journey of learning, revelation and insight. I've seen God at work in so many interesting and wonderful ways. As a result, I've come to know God in a much deeper and more intimate way; a way I would never have encountered if my life had been one of good health. It was God's help that has enabled me to write this book and share my experiences with others.

Writing this book has enabled me to see even more where God has been at work in my life. I have experienced all things working together for good. (*Romans 8:28,*) in each and every part of my journey, even if I haven't seen it at the time. He has molded and shaped me. *'Yet you, Lord, are our Father. We are the clay; you are the potter; we are all the work of your hand'. (Isaiah 64:8).*

What God has done for me is too much to put into words. He has saved me and chosen me to be in a relationship with Him. *'For he chose us in him before the creation of the world ...' (Ephesians 1:6).* He gave me the assurance that I will never die but live and go to be with Him in heaven and that's the biggest miracle I could ever hope for and everything else is an added bonus. I have to remind myself of this all the time.

It's easy to get anxious about the future, forgetting that God sees a bigger picture and is in control. In everything I try to remember and continue to trust that God has a plan and He is working it out for my good and His glory.

Writing this book has produced in me much emotional healing. I hadn't realised before just how much emotional pain can be carried as a result of dealing with ill health. I've been forced into a journey of reflection and deeper contemplation, without all of the confusion this time.

My health journey continues as I continue to fight the fight and be used for His glory. However, I don't allow sickness to define or defeat me. I make a daily choice to rise above it. Whatever circumstances I find myself in I have the assurance of knowing that God will carry me through. His grace is sufficient. I'd encourage you to bring your pain and grief to Him and allow Him to take your burdens.

I'd come to realise that even though some people can and do get supernaturally and instantly healed by God after receiving prayer, for others healing is a process that takes time, in some cases years. Even though Jesus doesn't heal everyone in the physical sense by removing all symptoms, He is always with us even at times when we don't realise it, comforting us, strengthening us and helping us through it all. His goodness is always there if we can only see it.

Throughout my journey of searching, I still don't have all the answers and I never will. Our human body, God, life in general is too complex to ever figure out fully. It's only the creator of all things that understands the complexity of our intricate design.

After much analysis and whilst trying to make sense of it all, I've reached the conclusion that sickness and lack of healing is a mystery beyond human comprehension. Even though I'm praying constantly for my healing, I have to face the possibility that I may be living with the symptoms of these health problems for the rest of my earthly life, but I will continue to trust in God and never give up praying and hoping that one day He will heal me fully. Even if it doesn't happen in my earthly lifetime, I've got the assurance of knowing that one day when I go to be with Jesus, this then will become a reality. *'He will wipe every tear from their eyes. There will be no more death' or mourning or crying or pain, for the old order of things has passed away,' (Revelation 21:4).*

<u>Recommended Websites I've used</u>

British Tinnitus Association <u>www.tinnitus.org.uk</u>
Central England Lipreading Support Trust
<u>www.celst.org.uk</u> for lipreading classes on zoom
Durham deafened Support <u>www.ddsupport.org.uk</u>
Fibromyalgia Action UK <u>www.fmauk.org</u>
Hearing Link <u>www.hearinglink.org</u>
Living Smarter with Fibromyalgia <u>www.living-smarter-with-fibromyalgia.com</u>
Mind <u>www.mind.org.uk</u>
NHS <u>www.nhs.uk</u> Health A-Z for symptoms,
causes, diagnosis, treatment, self-help.

Bibliography

APA PschNet. Psychological vulnerability and stress: The effects of self-affirmation on sympathetic nervous system responses to naturalistic stressors.
https://psycnet.apa.org/record/2009-14439-006

Babbs, Liz. *The Thing About Stress.* Lion Publishing, 2002

Dave Brandon, 22nd July. Our Daily Bread Ministries 2017 Volume 62.

Durrant-Peatfield, Barry. Your Thyroid and how to keep it healthy. Hammersmith Press Limited 2006, reprinted 2012

Gass, Bob & Debby. UCB Word for Today (Daily Devotional),Mar,Apr 2016, published by UCB

Gass, Bob & Debb. UCB Word for Today (Daily Devotional), Spring 2022, published by UCB

McLean, Andrea. Confessions of a Menopausal Woman

Prince, Derek. Blessing or Curse! You Can Choose! Published by Word (UK) 1990

Rubin, Jordan S N.M.D,Ph.D The Maker's Diet 2004, published by a Siloam.

Woolley, Fr John. I am with You. Divine Help For Today's Needs, 1984

Department of Gastroenterology, Monash University, Australia. the MONASH University Low
FODMAP diet Edition 4 2010.

Bible Gateway www.biblegateway.com (scriptures were quoted from here)

Goodreads Charles F Glassman.
www.goodreads.com

ibsnetwork   www.theibsnetwork.org

Inc. Why are those overly sensitive people who drive you crazy are actually gifted www.inc.com

National Academy of Hypothyroidism
www.nahypothroidism.org

NHS 5 Ways to Wellbeing www.nhs.uk

Oxford Languages www.languages.oup.com

Positive Psychology www.positivepsychology.com

Psychology Today www.psychologytoday.com

Social Anxiety Institute. What is social Anxiety?
www.socialanxietyinstitute.org

The worlds #1 website on hearing. Fibromyalgia increases the risk of hearing loss. www.hear-it.org

Verywell mind. What is a Highly Sensitive person (HSP) www.verywellmind.com

Martin, Penny, Inspired Christian Poetry

Printed in Great Britain
by Amazon